STREETERVILLE

STREETERVILLE

Chicago's Most Exciting Neighborhood

WAYNE KLATT

THE
History
PRESS

Published by The History Press
Charleston, SC
www.historypress.com

First published 2023

Manufactured in the United States

ISBN 9781467151573

Library of Congress Control Number: 2023937201

CONTENTS

INTRODUCTION

One summer dawn, I watched lights in some Streeterville offices come on as lake-facing windows reflected the colors of morning. Nearby apartments and condominiums turned bright one at a time from the lower levels up to what seemed like infinity. Hundreds of well-dressed men and women from these vertical homes would soon be riding down elevators and then up elevators to workplaces in the same community. Yet the crowded valley of bustle and tall buildings called Streeterville was once just lake, sand and dreams. Most of all, dreams.

For more than a century, what had been an untouched vastness cried out not for a building here and a building there but for ambitious master plans describing rows—blocks—half miles of developments so large they could only be built upward. The metamorphosis was unlike any other real estate speculation in the world. Just one man had envisioned it, quiet financier Potter Palmer, but for years, George Wellington Streeter insisted that he had created the acres with his own hands. If the courts had ruled in his favor, single ownership would now be worth incalculable billions. Incalculable, because Streeterville's value rises with every new tower.

Palmer's financial venture succeeded so well that the formerly shunned Near North Side drew the wealthy from the South Side, and later Lake Shore Drive mansions that were not very old were replaced by luxurious perpendicular residences. After a construction doldrums through the 1950s, new ideas spurred a Streeterville construction craze until the area blossomed with hotels and commercial suites alongside its residential spires. One never knew where a building would be refashioned or torn down for something taller.

For a while, Streeterville competed with the traditional business district, but by the 1990s, when people said "downtown" Chicago they meant trendy North Michigan Avenue and its lively little intersecting streets just across the river. Today the dreamers shaping the community are architects, investment bankers, foreign speculating groups and developers capable of vast conceptions. Ventures that fail make way for ones that succeed.

The genesis of this book came when I learned about the Streeter legend from my brother as a child, inspiring me years later as a newsman to delve into the area's secrets by discarding all previous accounts. My book *King of the Gold Coast* ended with Streeter's death at a time when the region was just coming into its own. While recovering from surgery in a hospital at the heart of Streeterville a decade later, I looked out at tall buildings that had not been there when the book came out and felt there was a need for the full story of a neighborhood that has been like no other.

Delving into the transformation of the boggy marsh goes into the genius of speculation, the venality of public officials and the doggedness of American individualism in times that had no use for it. Even though Streeter's name is on some buildings and is used in realty brochures, most men and women living or working in the area are unaware why they are not walking in sand and lake. The story includes secrecy, a fatal shooting, two murder trials and risks involving millions.

Little wonder Streeterville has become Chicago's most exciting community, not for its shopping and respectable nightlife but for the vibrancy of its residents and the vigor of its builders. Since this evolution cannot be understood without knowing the contrasting roles of Palmer and Streeter, I have condensed and rewritten the story told in the earlier book while expanding information about court cases and investigations, detailing the residential and commercial development from the beginning and adding accounts of rival claims to the shore as well as land creation ventures that have made the area what it is today. At the same time, I broadened the scope to encompass the complex development of the neighborhood from daydream to today's crowded panorama. The only photo here that appeared in the earlier book is one of Palmer's castle. And since speculators were not confined by neighborhood boundaries, in order to be inclusive, this book describes a few related projects across from Streeterville, such as Illinois Center.

Any account of the district runs into a confusion of similar names for buildings, and management companies tend to rename them when the trend changes. I identify contemporary buildings by their common name and use a single address when they are known by two. Every word in quoted matter is verbatim from its source, and no attempt has been made to standardize the phrasing.

Why should this one neighborhood need special treatment? Streeterville began with a secret arrangement between speculators and a state agency, yet the community and the Gold Coast that grew around it have economically strengthened the city and raised its status in the world. Even after years of familiarity with the facts, I still find it hard to believe that it all really happened.

PHASE ONE

THE VISION

We have always been a city of builders and dreamers.
—Mayor Richard M. Daley

1

Georg eorge Wellington Streeter was on trial for his life. In the winter of 1902, guards he had hired to protect his claim to the north shore of Chicago had shot it out with watchmen for the legitimate owners, and a young Missourian was killed just a few hundred yards from the new millionaires' district. Although witnesses were unable to say whether "Cap'n" Streeter had taken part in the shooting, one testified that the whiskery middle-aged man had instructed his watchmen to shoot anyone causing trouble, making him responsible. Yet the issue in this trial was not really Streeter's possible involvement but whether he had any claim to the land he was defending, which was turning into the most sought-after real estate between the coasts. Streeter had been telling whoppers for years about creating the Gold Coast with his own hands, and the legitimate owners were covering up secrets of their own. Because the lakeshore had never been adequately plotted, the validity of any ownership remained unclear, and court decisions were contradictory. To untangle the issues, we need to go back a little before the beginning.

NINE YEARS AFTER THE Great Fire of 1871, most of Chicago's wealthiest families lived around 18th and Prairie, a two-mile carriage ride to downtown offices and the better shops. British visitor William Stead noted, "Probably there are as many millions of dollars to the square inch of this residential

Cartoon police in a chase by Palmer's mansion. *Drawn by the author.*

district as are found in any equal on the world's surface." Yet at the time he wrote this, in 1893, some affluent families were shunning Prairie Avenue for mansions on what was then the stubby and denigrated Near North Side.

The inland portion was a growing Irish and Italian slum, with a few working-class and lower-middle-class homes on the edge, and on the lakeward side was a marsh once known as "The Sands." With the harbor nearby, the wasteland sported the worst kinds of prostitution until the cribs were torn down in 1857. Even a quarter of a century later, the barrenness was so tainted that the sandy shore discouraged nearly everyone except derelicts, fishermen and runaways. A few German families lived not far away, with the small Rush Street bridge their only link to the rest of the city. Sections of the marsh were cheap since there was no way to build permanent structures there.

The problem blocking northward expansion was that the city lies atop blue clay of compressed sediment left by an ancient lake, with pockets of quicksand and layers of trapped water below. In the 1870s, engineers worked out a new method for basing heavy loads on unsteady ground with the Eads Bridge in St. Louis. A succession of crisscrossing platforms of wrought iron and steel I-beams compacted the surface to such a density that the ground substituted for a foundation. But the achievement took its time reaching Chicago.

Rather than allowing the city's edge north of the harbor remain dunes and hallows, the State of Illinois authorized construction of long, narrow Lincoln Park as a buffer against Lake Michigan erosion. After the park's completion in 1875, the state designed a modest carriageway at the outer border and called it Lake Shore Drive. A ride along the park for those who could afford a buggy or carriage must have been a pleasurable escape from the smoke and mud of the city. But erosion persisted even after Lincoln Park commissioners widened the carriageway in 1880.

Several middle-class people by then had moved closer to the wilderness, largely along the undistinguished Pine Street. Pine looked nothing like it would when turned into the wide shopping street of North Michigan Avenue. With the attraction of the park nearby, some people bought shoreline lots and left them untouched in hopes that the marsh, created by spillover lake water, might someday give way to stores, saloons or factories, as with the rest of the growing city. Somehow. After severe storms, absentee owners rowed out with long poles "to assure themselves the [underwater] ground was still there," a newspaper noted. When respected Irish American portrait artist G.P.A. Healy went to register a piece of shore he had accepted as payment, a clerk told him, "But, Mr. Healy, it will cost you five dollars."

"I know that, that is the usual amount, isn't it?"

"Yes, but, you see, this land is under the lake!"[1]

He registered it anyway, and his heirs held onto it as its value rose into the millions, benefiting from the city's short-sightedness in neglecting the natural resource. Major cities from Boston to St. Petersburg, Russia, had turned their swamps into cityscapes, but Chicago authorities lacked vision and gave the area up to nature. After merchant and philanthropist John V. Farwell moved from the Prairie Avenue district to a short fashionable street adjacent to the North Side's Water Tower at Chicago Avenue, he must have thought he was putting something over on the park commission when he sold his nineteen acres of vacant shore for $5,000 an acre.

Elevators and telephones had changed the nature of running a corporation in the East, but the marsh and its mosquitoes forestalled any northward growth that would permit a new kind of company headquarters. Yet unlike real estate elsewhere, the shore kept growing by itself. In 1883, the chief engineer in Washington determined that the strand, as measured at an old city pier off Randolph Street, had crept nearly half a mile into the lake in just fourteen years. For those attuned to the opportunities of land development, the emptiness seemed to call for a bold plan that might turn silt and sand into gold. As Frederick Francis Cook observed in *Bygone Days of Chicago*, "In no other American centre of architecture was the struggle quite so intense or so full of hazards, because of the city's rapid growth and the persistent lure of schemes of development far ahead of their time of fruition. Land, not manufactures, was the accepted road to riches. Therefore, whatever was undertaken was usually with an eye to increase land values."[2]

Potter Palmer, who reshaped modern Chicago with State Street and Lake Shore Drive. *Chicago History Museum.*

The only person with a mind quick enough to discern a way mansions could be built on the unsteady surface was hotel owner and shrewd speculator Potter Palmer. The six-foot Quaker from New York State was so self-contained that he dominated any room without presenting himself as the leader. He saw the stretch of nothing as a chance to turn Chicago in a new direction, literally. He must have felt that the merchant class was being strangled by streetcar lines, railroad tracks, common apartment buildings and slapdash single housing surrounding the city's three upscale residential districts: South Prairie Avenue, South Ashland Boulevard and West Washington Street.

The solution was tied in with the city's love for railroads. Of the twenty-six lines using half a dozen terminals, only the Illinois Central had the clout to cross downtown and reach the river warehouses. But for the people living at 18th and Prairie, it meant that the swirling black smoke heaved from locomotives destroyed their air and disrupted their tranquility. Although the I-C was compelled to erect a brick wall between its tracks and the millionaire district, stately marble homes that were originally white soon turned a dirty gray that could not be scrubbed away. Palmer must have thought that the elite deserved better—deserved, in fact, an entirely new district of fresh air and exclusivity. One built on landfill, like the downtown train tracks.

Palmer's mind worked like no other influential person's in the city. He had realized his gift for sensing future needs when he bought all the cotton he could at the outbreak of the Civil War to sell for Union uniforms. Soon after arriving in Chicago years later, he could see that the energetic mud pit of a city was growing in the wrong direction. The main stores ran east and west along a river whose mouth had been dredged into a halfway adequate harbor. Millinery shops stood near docks where begrimed workmen in their muddy boots continually loaded and unloaded cargo.

Not yet able to do anything about it, Palmer built a major dry goods store on Lake Street, next to the curving river, and instituted a "no questions asked" return policy. Already successful from his investments, he worked such long workdays at the store that doctors advised him to take a rest. He sold the business to Marshall Field and sailed to Europe. Friends must have doubted Palmer's sanity when upon his return he bought up $1 million worth of downtown land along narrow, north- and south-running State Road. At the northern end of this quarter mile, he erected his Palmer House hotel, a wedding present for his wife. But the Great Fire the next year leveled it along with most of the city.

Without the devastation, Chicago might have developed without a plan like Buffalo and St. Louis. Instead of rebuilding the city, merchants and laborers built a new one as soon as the ruins were carted away. Palmer ceded the western stretch of renamed State Street to the city so that it could be widened into a fashionable thoroughfare. He then leased the entire frontage facing the lake to important retailers, in time creating a great American bazaar. The concentration of shops, theaters and business concerns around State Street became known across the country as the Loop because of the streetcars and elevated trains circling around it.

Yet Chicago lagged behind New York City in elegant living. The nouveau riche in Manhattan paid high rents for apartments with amenities and servant quarters, and the structures were managed by cooperative associations to ensure high standards. But the affluent in Chicago were prejudiced against large apartment buildings, equating them with slum tenements. Palmer and his wealthy poker-playing friends must have sensed that if they waited until attitudes changed before speculating in the shore, there would be ill-considered building projects everywhere. And the only way to control the development would be to buy up the entire marsh and fringe areas, if possible.

The conception of transforming the wasteland did not visit Palmer some night as he slept in his hotel. The starting point may have been when Judge Murray Tuley suggested sometime around 1881 that the city's eastern limit of homes and businesses just north of the river, Sand Street (now St. Clair Street), might be enhanced with some sort of Lincoln Park Commission landfill. Tuley may have been thinking of just a park extension, but Palmer

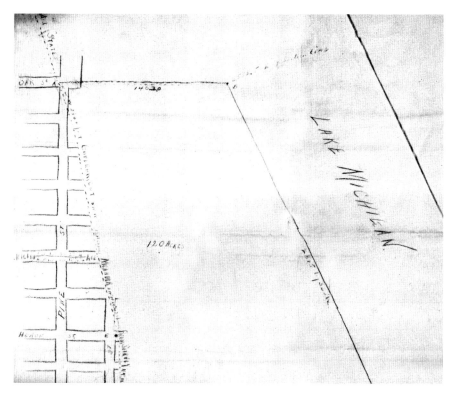

A very faint map of the Streeterville wasteland. *Chicago History Museum.*

could see the park carriageway crossing a reclaimed shore for a row of mansions built with Eads Bridge–style platforms.

The only eyewitness account we have of Palmer's instigating the plan comes from a friend who recalled much later that Potter once casually said, "I'm going over there, north, to work out a new residence district." A companion joked that "it would slip into the lake." His grand scheme may have spun off from an even earlier idea. German immigrant Tobias Allmendinger once suggested that the city consider protecting empty north shore property like his with a somewhat elevated street that would protect it from crashing waves.

But a millionaires' row was only the first phase of his vision. Intuition told him that the real fortunes would be made, as in Manhattan, from high rises designed for new-moneyed people and for men and women tired of living in piles of stone. With stunning clarity, he could advance this idea for twenty or thirty years. However, Palmer needed to act quickly, because Roman Catholic bishop Patrick Feehan had a parallel dream for exploiting the shore.

The prelate had turned an old archdiocese cemetery near the park into an upscale district eventually called Astor Street. Architects came up with handsome Queen Anne–style townhouses without a shadow between them and without a boulevard to lend them beauty. Astor Street drew a number of the well-off but failed to interest what society considered the best families. Bishop Feehan could have blocked a portion of Lake Shore Drive, but he would let it be built across part of the abandoned cemetery when Palmer agreed to finance a private sewer to improve Astor drainage.[3]

As first conceived, Palmer's venture would reclaim a total of ninety-three acres of submerged land and fill in an unknown wider area above the surface.[4] The unprecedented project would have succumbed to practicalities were it not for what is known as the Chicago Way. Behind the boosterism about its being the fastest-growing city in the world was a back alley of bribery in which the upright caved in to expediency. Zoning changes and reinterpretations of real estate laws, however warranted, were impossible unless public officials received something under the table. This was the way the city worked; this was what made Chicago great in America's Gilded Age.

Our understanding of the scheme comes solely from the sequence of events, a few obscure names on city plats and insinuations at legislative hearings. What these show is that rather than being a simple enterprise such as Astor Street, Palmer's conception involved two simultaneous stages, both requiring discretion. To begin, as Chicago's leading citizen Palmer would build the first mansion on the marsh whether he wanted to live there or not. Acquiring nearby land would be conducted surreptitiously through straw purchasers; otherwise, rival investors would pounce on any hint the visionary was buying up lots. All transfer of property would be protected by land trusts, as devised by the Chicago Title and Trust Company and then used nationwide. The tricky—and illegal—second stage would be to persuade the Lincoln Park Commission, answerable only to the state, to extend its carriageway without public notice that tax money would support a massive private enterprise.

While confidential discussions were being conducted toward eventually acquiring the entire shore from the river to the park, work began in 1882 on what seemed a solitary and foolish venture, Palmer's home on the sand land. For his residence in the middle of nowhere, he called for something unheard of, an American castle. The design was of a large but ordinary stone house from which a castellated tower rose, its archaic ornamentation in keeping with the respected Water Tower.

When work went from just scooping up and spreading sand to filling in swampy dips, the *Chicago Tribune* noted that "garbage laden with germs is dumped day by day on made land at Superior Street." In a single day, a reporter counted twenty-seven double-teamed wagons unloading cinders, kitchen garbage and sweepings from butcher shops and stables in violation of ordinances permitting only ashes and dry dirt. Bishop Feehan became hot around the turned-around collar when contractors working for the park commission failed to smooth out the landfill on either side of the carriageway route, leaving a scrubby landscape.[5]

With Palmer's demands, his castle proved five years in the construction. In that period, what documents called the Ohio Street Extension was well underway. Though the eastern edge of the city ended at Sand Street (St. Clair), without public notification or explanation, the obliging common council of aldermen in 1885 extended Oak from Sand Street to the Drive route and in 1887 built Chestnut Street across the made land, perhaps to facilitate crews working on the Drive and building future manses.[6]

While Palmer awaited completion of his stone home, a French Renaissance–style mansion went up in 1883 on the marsh off Bellevue Place

Palmer's "castle" still divides opinion between classic beauty and ludicrous imitation. *Author's collection.*

for attorney and civil engineer William Borden, whose millions had come from Colorado silver mines. By choosing Borden, Palmer was showing the skeptical that this was the type of resident who would be living in the once-scorned area. In fact, Borden's son would die of a disease contracted while serving as a missionary in China.

Also in 1883, caissons were laid off Bellevue at what would be 88 Lake Shore Drive, later number 1000, for Chicago Board of Trade member Nathaniel Jones. The palatial forty-one-room chateau was sold to Harold McCormick of the prosperous reaper family and his wife, Edith, of the Standard Oil Rockefellers. After their divorce, Edith remained in the mansion as a society matron rivaling Bertha Palmer, and Harold underwent a nonhuman gland transplant—reportedly from a goat—and enjoyed the company of a younger woman. Construction also began in 1883 for the grindstone home of attorney Franklin McVeagh, future U.S. Treasury secretary. His mansion at 103 Lake Shore Drive (later 1400) was topped by a French-style mansard roof and had such a Bastille look that a newspaper called living there "luxurious imprisonment." The structure was constructed immediately north of Potter's castle site, with a breakwater and narrow shoulder of sand linking them.

Palmer could only blame himself for delays that had kept him from being the first resident. When he was presented with plans for a $90,000 house, he outlined what he wanted and reportedly told the architects, "Do not show me the final reckoning." The result looked like half Tower of London and half fish tank toy. It rose slowly from caissons secured below twelve feet of pure landfill and watery sand, and it would take at least two years to settle. The fortress-like residence was so exclusive that it was constructed without exterior locks, since admittance would be only by servant. An architectural critic termed the Palmer home "the mansion to end all mansions," but Chicago novelist Arthur Meeker considered it "a monstrosity." Palmer was honored with the address of 100 Lake Shore Drive, later changed to 1350.

In early 1885, Potter and Bertha Palmer went by lacquered carriage to their new home, and servants welcomed them inside. It was said that once the Palmers were "receiving," a visitor's card passed through the hands of twenty-seven butlers, maids and social secretaries before a gentleman was admitted. The visitor would have seen the self-conscious luxury of Oriental rugs, Venetian mosaics and tiger skins in one room and stained-glass windows and a coat of arms from Bertha's French lineage in another. The chambers were oak-bound caverns, and the dining room

The Edith McCormick mansion, 1910. This was considered the height in single-family residences through the 1920s. *Chicago History Museum.*

could accommodate fifty guests. Roman busts stared blankly, chandeliers hung obtrusively and everywhere small electric lights in white globes compensated for heavy drapery blocking the sun. Potter relaxed with friends in the masculinity of his library and billiard room, and when alone on nights he was not staying at his hotel suite, he preferred his bedroom in the tower.[7]

The bed in Honore's room had blue taffeta curtains. Mrs. Palmer conceived Chicago's New Year's Day charity ball, starting in 1886. At all large gatherings, she set the standard for relaxed decorum and polite amusements for society matrons and their business-minded husbands. Once carriage drivers took them away, there was just solitude and lapping waves. But the purpose of the Drive had now come into focus. With the two Bellevue mansions on the northern end of the Drive route and Potter's castle on the southern, the configuration virtually cried out for monied citizens to relocate between them.

The collusion making all this possible is evident. Lake Shore Drive planners had needed a civil engineer to carry out the extensive landfill to not only make the marsh disappear but also persuade the park commission

Interior of Palmer's mansion, considered the most elegant home in Chicago in the 1890s. *Chicago History Museum.*

to extend its carriageway. Chosen was Charles Fitz-Simons, who had built bridges for the Union army and whose dredging company opened in Chicago a year after the Great Fire. Tall Fitz-Simons had the kind of paunch expected in successful men. Fond of uniforms and parades, he formerly headed the Illinois National Guard. But he might have been involved from the beginning. If Allmendinger had told him his idea for an elevated street,

Fitz-Simons could have relayed this to Palmer. But what we have points to Palmer as being the originator.

To buy nearby empty lots owned by assorted individuals, Palmer's insider friends joined investors from DeKalb County, Illinois, to set up the North Side Land Association. Incorporating let purchasers keep their names off legal documents. The association offered capital stock at $500,000, divided into $100 shares. The easy money enticed many wasteland lot owners to sell, unaware how valuable the property would become. The Chicago Title and Trust Company, enjoying a monopoly on property records ever since the Great Fire, took over title to each acquired lot as trustee. The association then merged with the Pine Street Land Association to represent middle-class residents and property owners of that still-ordinary street. With this union, Palmer's plan gained scope by expanding the burgeoning Gold Coast several blocks westward and making possible the eventual transformation of Pine Street into North Michigan Avenue.[8]

Once individuals in the park commission agreed privately to support Palmer's venture, the agency handpicked wealthy men for a citizens committee to determine whether extending the drive across the virtually worthless shore would benefit the public—a foregone conclusion. The new owners concealed their interests by hiring attorney H.F. Shelton to front for them. Possibly he was the one who persuaded the two most respected North Siders, retired attorney Franklin MacVeagh and Judge Lambert Tree, to appear before Illinois legislators in support of the extension. Unaware of the underlying real estate project, MacVeagh and Judge Tree saw only civic improvement and health benefits in a shoreline road that would bring relief from smoky factories and summer heat.[9]

Only an already corrupt agency could have embarked on the project without public attention. Commission Superintendent William C. Goudy was often by Palmer's elbow at Illinois Club card tables and, as a lawyer, was known for pressing moneyed interests through the courts. But his shady dealings had led liberal governor John Peter Altgeld to disassociate himself from his friend. Quite possibly, Palmer had counted on Goudy's complicity when he conceived of the millionaires' district. Approval was such a sure thing that the state enabling bill was drafted on behalf of several people with a personal interest in its passage, including N.K. Fairbank.

For a century, most Chicagoans were unaware of Palmer's Genesis-like role in the creation of the Gold Coast. But after his death, his family wanted to imagine that he had done everything by himself, as shown by these excerpts from private memorials on file at the Chicago History Museum:

[T]*he north shore seemed destined to be covered with palaces and villas, parks and pleasure grounds for public and private uses. A boulevard along the north shore would provide axcess* [sic] *to these beauties of art and nature combined. Mr. Palmer saw in such a frontage the possibilities of a new and much needed residence section....Mr. Palmer immediately employed dredges and pumped the clean lake sand from the bed of the lake into vacant property, which was thus filled with absolutely clean and wholesome sand and formed an admirable foundation for the structure* [his castle].

He purchased the waste in large quantities [and] *encouraged the Lincoln Park Commission to come southward* [from the park].... *The lake front was filled in, the waste space utilized, the drive laid out and ornamented* [landscaped], *the side streets cut through, a new residence neighborhood created and thus was added to the city new values and the most beautiful and popular and greatly needed residence quarter of Chicago....This required some one person who had large property interests, that the work might be well and properly done.*

Just when the plan was beginning to stall, the final middle-class owner of a sizable portion of lake-washed land, Tobias Allmendinger, needed ready cash. General Fitz-Simons first bought two lots from a fellow Alliance member for $35,000 and paid off the $30,000 mortgage. This gave him credibility for telling Allmendinger he wished to expand his holdings. On January 6, 1886, Allmendinger agreed to sell a lot between Walton and Pearson for $75,000. Because the immigrant may have been the first to suggest protecting shore lands with a raised street, for a while, Fitz-Simons let it be thought the German had originated the entire Lake Shore Drive project.[10]

Impatient Fitz-Simons signed preliminary contracts for Drive construction in 1886 while the enabling bill was still under consideration. Neighbors still had no idea why noisy dredging equipment was creeping off the shore and the marsh. Pine Street residents even petitioned the Illinois attorney general in August, complaining of work being done between Oak and Pearson "for the purpose of enclosing for private use some 13 acres of submerged land," their attorney said. "North shore residents with property near the lake are at this time also interested in a mysterious line of piles [pilings]." They received no explanation.[11]

All-important discussions among commissioners on whether to create Lake Shore Drive and the rest of the Gold Coast were held clandestinely.

The Illinois attorney's office would charge that Fitz-Simons appeared at several of the sessions to encourage the project. Approval was ensured because Superintendent Goudy was an aggressive real estate speculator who ran the agency without a full accounting, as a legislative investigation would show. No one outside the park commission and the circle of investors knew an extension was even being considered. Park commissioners conveniently neglected to mention the enormous expenditures to the taxpayers until there was a brief acknowledgement under pressure in September 1892, nearly a decade after the fact. Details were not given until the next year, and then only as listings in an annual report.[12]

2

F ew people are hurled into history more dramatically than George Wellington Streeter. In his account, he helmed a forty-foot excursion boat through high lake waves after a gale struck on Saturday afternoon, July 10, 1886. He was in his forties, red-bearded to cover a weak chin and sinewy. Streeter claimed that he had been hazarding his craft to test it for gun-running to Roatán, an island off the coast of politically unstable Honduras. The Cap'n—the title was self-applied and he never wrote it down, so the appellation is sometimes given as "Cap" or "Capt."—said that swells knocked him overboard twice but he clambered back as his wife remained below. At around 10:00 p.m., the leaky steamboat supposedly split on a sandbar eight hundred feet out, near the landmark Water Tower at Chicago Avenue, and drifted about four hundred feet overnight into shallow water offshore.

But does anything in Streeter's background suggest he was capable of such planning and endurance? Scanty evidence suggests he was the black sheep of a large farm family near Flint, Michigan, preferring as a boy to play with the local Indians rather than apply himself to study or farmwork. After a rudimentary education, young George ran away, only to fail at everything he tried, whether it was owning a circus, running an Iowa hotel or, so he said, prospecting out West. He was conscripted into the Union army but, seeing no need to stay after the Civil War ended, deserted. What we are sure about him is that he was a liar, storyteller, schemer and con man—yet shrewd enough to stand up to some of the city's best families.

The Cap'n said he was born in 1837, but a census taken a year before the Civil War, military records, a marriage certificate and the variety of tales he told indicate that he first saw light a few years afterward. Whatever the year was, his birthday was June 11. A wishful thinker, he told the army he was a shipbuilder. Records show that Streeter never saw battle, though he may have exchanged shots with Rebel stragglers, and his supposed wartime injuries were just "piles" (hemorrhoids) as well as back sores from the swaying of his knapsack at a time when discipline often involved marching with rocks in the slacker's pack. A bullet wound in his lower leg that he often claimed came from a Confederate rifle may have been from a civilian encounter.[13]

In between failed enterprises, he married seventeen-year-old Lavina "Minnie" Waters in Michigan in 1876, when he was thirty-two to thirty-six. On his marriage registration, he listed his occupation as attorney. Minnie "decamped suddenly without notice, carrying with her my hard-earned cash," he told a friend. Streeter claimed he obtained a divorce. The Cap'n then traveled back and forth between Illinois and Indiana looking for an opportunity. By 1885, he had hooked up with Mary "Maria" Mulholland, a plain-faced, dumpy woman who dressed like a farmer's wife although her Irish Catholic father had served in the British army. Maria's gusto, her coarse way of speaking her mind and her readiness to use anything at hand to defend her husband's property made her a perfect match for the Cap'n, a backsliding Methodist. "She was fightin' Irish, scared o' nothin'," he would say.

The Streeters lived in a shack at a Calumet River shipyard off 95th Street, on the Far South Side. The Cap'n patched up an old steamboat that he named or said he named the *Reutan*. Unlike his fanciful tale of planning to run guns, he more likely wanted to operate the vessel as a "bum boat" that would sell alcohol on Sundays, when land sales were illegal, and possibly accommodate prostitution, as with two similar boats that had operated off Chicago's Randolph Street. In the book he co-wrote about his life, the Cap'n made sure events that crashed him and Maria against the watery northern edge of Chicago remained unclear.

Among the secret new owners of the windy shore was the Newberry family, which had become wealthy from banking, shipping and real estate. A watchman named Dugan was alarmed when daylight on July 11 revealed a drenched couple in a ruptured craft, their detached lifeboat making it to shore without them. In Streeter's telling, they were 450 feet from shore. Perhaps, but the closest charted sandbar was nearer the river mouth. Young De Witt Cregier Jr., son of the city engineer, showed up on the shore. The

Cregiers were among the middle-class people living around St. Clair Street, the boundary between the developed city and the marsh. Maybe he wanted to see if his family's holdings had survived the storm. He helped the Cap'n push the ruins to the sandy slope.

Somehow, Fitz-Simons appeared. "I was working as a contractor on shore when I noticed a little sloop being poled to the shore by a red-whiskered man," Fitz-Simons related to jurors in Streeter's first murder trial. "I saw that he intended to tie up at the Farwell pier. I went out to the pier and, as he came alongside, I notified him not to make fast there, as it was a private landing and I was in charge of it. He paid no attention to me."

Why would Fitz-Simons be "working as a contractor on shore" on a Sunday morning in those Sabbath-abiding times unless he was looking after his investment? And why would he be "in charge of" an area around Farwell's pier? That portion now belonged to the state, since the merchant had ceded his riparian rights for the construction of the Drive. So some of his testimony was a lie; but if he was right about Streeter poling to the land, that would mean the *Reutan* was not as badly damaged as the Cap'n would claim afterward.

Since only a handful of insiders knew the purpose of filling in the shore, how could this bloviating failure know that something shady was going on? Fitz-Simons was a blustery, high-keyed man who wrote indignant letters to editors. Whatever he blurted out, or almost blurted out, Streeter's underrated canniness took over. The contractor's overreaction, the road pilings, Palmer's castle, three other new mansions—it must have added up. Now or over the next few days, the Cap'n must have thought that if he could lump whatever was available onto the reclaimed marsh, he might get away with insisting that he had created the landfill beneath it. He would begin by building a tiny island around his wreckage. But how might he claim ownership? As a deserter, he was unable to take advantage of a government program granting unclaimed land to Union army veterans. But veterans' widows qualified, and Maria's late husband had served in the war.

Prosecutors in the first murder trial alleged that after Streeter was warned off Farwell's land, known as Block 1, Cregier helped him pole to shore and push the ruins up adjacent wet sand belonging to Fairbank, owner of Block 2. The Cap'n asked Fairbank or his agent for the temporary use of the plot to repair his boat. The millionaire let him. But instead of making the boat sailable, Streeter "became an intolerable nuisance" by staying, a newspaper claimed. "I discovered that sand had drifted and backed up considerably" behind the boat, Streeter said, through the words of his collaborator. "I concluded that I would build up a rock wall on the sea side of the boat and then aid the deposit."[14]

The Cap'n paid garbage wagon drivers fifty cents per load to deposit their haul off Superior Street, then put together a "yawl" propelled by push poles to shuttle refuse between the mainland and the sandbar. He surrounded the split hull with tons of silt, sand and such construction debris as broken bricks, heavy paving stones and discarded chunks of marble and sandstone. The Cap'n insisted he did the loading and unloading alone, but a friend reported that he hired roustabouts. Whoever supplied the muscle, the hasty dumping daily raised the ruined boat and Streeter's hopes. The little island emerged from the lake as late November gusts blew in from Canada.[15] The work was conducted in full view of the occasional policeman who showed up to discourage hobos, drunks and hookers from staying on the wasteland.

Streeter also must have been excitedly spreading detritus over the professional landfill for the emerging millionaires' district. No one suspected that the couple might remain for years where they weren't wanted, not even Farwell and Fairbank, the city's cultural leader. In *Captain Streeter, Pioneer*, the Cap'n included Farwell among the "dollar hogs," but in his young manhood, John V. donated half his salary to the Methodist Church.

Just because Streeter's land claims were bogus did not mean that Fairbank, Farwell and others held their deeds legally. The conflict stems from an oversight in an 1821 survey by engineer John Wall. He recorded a dividing line between land and lake but failed to specify whether it was a boundary or just a meander line. Lake levels changed cyclically by the year, and the unprotected shoreline was reshaped with every gale. A meander line marked where the shore was only at the time of the survey, the boundary subject to change at the whim of nature.[16] This ambiguity caused enough confusion to accommodate every assertion of ownership.

The *Reutan* could not have withstood many winters, and so the Streeters must have been glad when high winds blew a hulk toward shore in early 1888. The couple so successfully converted it into a home that it would later be mistaken for a barn. This second "scow" was about thirty feet long and had the ground for a floor. Streeter tarred the overhead oak planks as weatherproofing, and a large opening in the stern led to a "back porch" facing the route for Lake Shore Drive.[17]

After two years, Fairbank, owner of a nationally advertised lard and soap company, could tolerate the Streeters no longer. He rode onto the disputed property sometime around 1889, and the Cap'n climbed down the boat ladder with a rifle or shotgun to greet him. He was joined by a white bulldog or bull terrier named Spot, as all his dogs were. Scowling at him by his carriage was a fairly good-looking man in his early fifties, a founder of the Chicago Public Library and one of the largest contributors to charities and cultural causes in the city. The Cap'n must have asked something like, "What do you want?" because Fairbank told him: "I want you to get off my land, that's what I want, and I'm giving you exactly twenty-four hours to get out!"

"This is my land and I'm going to stay here until hell freezes over," Streeter snapped.

Fairbank then filed a forcible detainer (eviction) suit to move the couple off his vacant property, but nothing came of it even though there was no doubt the Cap'n was just a squatter. A law stated that no one could "obtain title to soil upon which" shoreline landfill was laid without state authorization. Streeter originally said he had created 4 acres off Superior, but with accretions and imagination, he eventually adjusted this to 186 acres, the approximate size of the marsh.

The codger was clearly waiting to be bought off, but the secret new owners refused to play his game. So the middle-class owners of sandland lots, most of them living around St. Clair or Pine Street, started hectoring Streeter with security guards and demanding action from city officials. Referring to this period, the Cap'n said, "They asked the Health Department to fire me, and I fired the Health Department. They sent the harbormaster to put me off, an' that didn't work. Mr. Fairbank, he said he'd burn me off, an' I said I'd shoot Mr. Fairbank's whiskers off if he dared try it." As the Cap'n told his lawyer-friend Francis X. Busch, "There ain't no law kin touch me. This is my land, and I'll kill any son of a bitch what says it ain't."

Fairbank's agents kept up the harassment by filing writs in justice of the peace courts. Park commission attorney Edward O. Brown denied that Fairbank and the others used only the lowest courts against Streeter because they feared an ultimate ruling by the Illinois Supreme Court. But what other explanation is there?

3

We speak of the North Side at this time as if it were larger than it was. With the marsh blocking the way, the only reason Chicago came as far north as Ohio Street was that health officials needed remote locations for quarantine stations and two hospitals during an 1852 cholera epidemic. After that, the common council had little use for the fifty-nine acres it had bought for less than $9,000, and so nearly all construction occurred on the South and West Sides.[18]

Nearly a decade after the Great Fire, the state authorized special districts for infrastructure improvements by local taxing bodies, making the carriageway extension feasible. Even though the park commission had no legal right to construct anything else on parkland, landfill under a route plotted by T.H. Handbury of the U. S. Corps of Engineers progressed across the North Side stub of the city and continued through the independently governed and contiguous North and Lake View Townships.[19] But changes needed to be made to the accepted route, and Superintendent Goudy persuaded the legislature to pass a bill allowing concessions to the shore owners. Attorney Shelton, representing the property owners, appeared uneasy at a state senate hearing years later when asked if it was true the owners would not sign contracts until the route "was fixed to suit them"—that is, built farther into the lake to give them more landfill property. "Yes, certainly," he replied, "exactly." In violation of municipal and Illinois law, the commission never advertised for construction bids.[20]

Each owner of shoreline property who gave up his riparian rights received a state deed that was placed in escrow until all questions could be settled. Once this was done, crews deposited landfill over an area from the adjusted offshore route west to St. Clair. Workmen also smoothed out land for future residences along the Drive and for which, the *Chicago Tribune* charged, the contractor had no permit.[21] Pilings were cut at an even level just below the surface, and on this base was laid a platform of three-inch oak planks. Through representatives, owners agreed to pay for their landfill at an estimated rate of $100 per running foot. In return, the park commission promised to build a breakwater when it had enough money.

Fitz-Simons's men built concrete blocks for the breakwater five years before the General Assembly passed the Lake Shore Drive enabling bill. In late 1886, the ten-ton blocks were laid to support a carriageway from Indiana Street (the downtown portion of Grand Avenue) north to Bellevue Place. Brown, the authority on shoreline issues, alleged in a 1902 report on the formerly submerged real estate "that an unconscionable advantage had been taken of the public by the shore owners, and that many millions of dollars worth of property had been obtained for the expenditure of possibly a million."[22] As late as 1899, not one of the wealthy owners had paid the $100 per running foot, and the park commission had to vote for additional funds to finish construction. By then the developed portion of the wasteland was on its way toward becoming a community, with members of the Palmer, McCormick and Medill families volunteering as street and alley inspectors to keep their ward clean.

When the route was smoothed, teams laid a wide temporary carriage path of planking resembling a boardwalk and landscaped both sides with a thin border of trees. As the road crept toward Cedar, it was accompanied by a bicycle path and paved beach of marble blocks to resist waves as the city finally began taming nature. The Drive was turning out so well that Palmer considered expanding the elite district all the way inland to Pine. Like the streets around it, Pine in the mid-1880s seemed hardly more than a narrow and badly paved alley. A newspaper called it "an ignoble lane" where horse-drawn wagons jounced and jostled past shacks, commonplace low-rise apartments and rubbish heaps.

Brown said reclaiming the shore had produced "a sort of no-man's land, teeming with potential wealth beyond the dreams of avarice."[23] In keeping with Palmer's greater vision, the Chicago Title and Trust Company took over from the Pine Street Land Association, putting all shore owners under single representation and maintaining a small army of lawyers to fight off challenges as they came along. When Lake Shore Drive was widened from Pearson Street to Bellevue Place, feeder streets became prime real estate.

4

More members of Chicago's fragmented society sought to relocate to the incomplete Lake Shore Drive than Potter Palmer would allow. Residence in these early years was by invitation, and in 1887, he welcomed President Lincoln's surviving son, Robert Todd Lincoln. He built a grim stone mansion at 60 Lake Shore Drive, later numbered 1234. Robert Todd was brilliant but calculating rather than gregarious. He earlier had his mother, Mary, institutionalized mainly because her continual talk of money and clothes embarrassed him. As a corporate lawyer, his riches derived from taking a board membership of whatever business he represented, including Commonwealth Edison, the Commercial Bank and the Pullman railroad car company.

Crews were still driving pilings into navigable water down to twelve feet. The carriageway originally had a narrow channel running along the shore, but after several years, this was covered over and there is no trace of it. Meanwhile, the area north of the river was growing geographically. In 1889, Chicago annexed the town of Lake View, followed by adjacent North Township in 1902, creating a large North Side.

So far, the secret land grab by some of the city's finest citizens had gone smoothly. But Park Commission member Horatio May, son of a doctor and a conscientious public servant, was strolling by Bellevue Place in the spring of 1892 when he noticed something odd at the foot of Oak Street. It was "as if the piles were away beyond the line," a newspaper reported. In fact, the pilings had been pounded 135 to 150 feet farther out than they should have been. As would be learned later, that section was pledged to the contractor who had installed them, General Fitz-Simons. His role in the plan was so shady that he did not receive his deed until the project passed legislative scrutiny so that at any inquiry he could claim disinterest in the project.[24]

When former park superintendent Joseph Stockton, now just a member of the agency, was asked why the commission had made changes in the route to satisfy the shore owners, he explained, "We had a good deal of trouble in getting all the owners to consent to the arrangement, and it seemed to be the best way to get the improvements made," meaning construction of the carriageway. Stockton was ousted as superintendent because Governor Altgeld considered him corrupt.[25]

The lawmakers learned that former commission secretary John Taylor was virtually doubling his wages by charging extra fees for commission work and that Superintendent Pettigrew was pocketing some profits from food, drinks and souvenirs sold in the park. The senators were even more surprised that commission meetings were held virtually in secret and with few notes taken. Stockton and two former park commissioners testified they had no knowledge of large expenditures or other matters related to the extension, "except," the *Chicago Tribune* noted, "what the superintendent [the late Goudy] chose to tell them."[26] Despite suspicions of collusion, the park commission continued to withhold the identities of shore owners until the senators subpoenaed them, and even then the list it submitted was incomplete:

Indiana Street (Grand Avenue) to Ohio Street: the McCormick and Ogden estates;

Ohio to Ontario Street: the Ogden estate;

Ontario to Erie Street: the Ogden estate and several unnamed individuals;

Erie to Huron Street: shared by the Newberry estate; Maria Smith, Walter Newberry's daughter; Potter Palmer; Horace Hurlbut of the J.H. Reed Company; and unnamed others;

Huron to Superior Street: Fairbank and the Newberry estate;

Superior to Chicago Avenue: John V. Farwell;

(Chicago Avenue to Pearson Street was city land surrounding the Water Tower)

Pearson to Chestnut Street: the Cregiers;

Walton to Chestnut Street: George Edward Rickords of the Chicago Title and Trust Company;

Chestnut to Oak Street: no ownership was given, but half a dozen entities and citizens including Fitz-Simons were listed as being "interested."

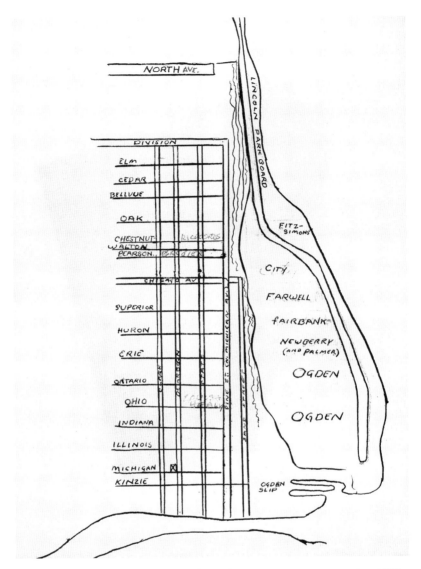

Informal map of Streeterville showing formerly secret property owners, circa 1890. *Drawn by the author as a memory aid.*

The list curiously did not continue for land at Bellevue and Cedar.

The Bartling Committee concluded that the Drive extension was a "theft from the navigable waters of Lake Michigan" and the carriageway "leads nowhere and is valuable only to the abutting and contiguous property owners as an exit from the made land." The lawmakers further charged that "the property owners by undue influence of some sort [bribery] used the Lincoln Park Commissioners" to advance their interests. The panel further charged that the road was essentially a private driveway for the rich whose message to the working class was, in their words, "Keep off the grass." They may have refrained from recommending legal action because they concurred with Shelton when he told them, "When we are under the daisies, future generations will enjoy the fruits of our labor in making the Shore Drive."[27]

The illegal pilings were allowed to remain, and the sweeping bulge of Oak Street remains today as a major beach. As for Streeter, the lawmakers said he had lost any legitimate claim to land accruing around his old boat by dumping around it. The outed shore owners were so relieved that their enterprise had survived legislative scrutiny that in November they sought to rename the Drive "Palmer Boulevard." Potter was mortified, not only because he was an extremely private person but also because linking him to the project would shatter the impression that shore ownership was a matter of individual purchases.[28]

There was some question about whether the outer pilings fell under state or federal jurisdiction, since they were in navigable waters for shallow-draft boats. On May 26, 1894, the U.S. Supreme Court ruled that state authority extended to the section including the waters off land Palmer and his agents had purchased. Feisty Illinois attorney general Maurice Moloney used the decision to sue the owners as well as Fitz-Simons and the park commission to cancel all contracts. He actually wanted to rip up Lake Shore Drive and restore the land to lake and marsh. Walrus-like Fitz-Simons responded by entering Moloney's Chicago office and, according to one account, throwing a fist at him, but Moloney ducked.[29]

In November, the Illinois attorney general set up charts and maps behind Circuit Court judge Thomas Wendes to prove that the former swampy area had been illegally converted, in that the farthest pilings went twelve to fourteen feet below the surface. The Irishman also wanted to show that Fitz-Simons had signed a preliminary contract for the Drive three years before the state authorized construction, but Judge Wendes dismissed that as irrelevant. Next, attorney Sheldon presented himself as originator of the plan. His falsehoods were so muddled that he claimed the idea came to him in 1887, four years after mansions started going up. The judge had heard enough and threw out the suit in January 1895. Wasting no time, the Illinois Supreme Court that same month upheld his decision, and Lake Shore Drive continued past Cedar.

5

Visitors to Chicago for the dazzling Columbian Exposition may have been dismayed by the city's unfinished look. Buildings close to the polluted river were on stilts to avoid flooding, and the air was thick with factory and locomotive smoke, contributing to what a guidebook called "pallid faces, faltering steps, lassitude." Companies took to dumping garbage and rubble off a pier at Ohio Street, leading people to refer to that smelly area as "Piertown." Unaware of Palmer's secretive real estate venture, the *Chicago Herald* questioned why Fitz-Simons's crews had been "engaged for years" in dumping refuse landfill off Superior. By February 1894, the heap covered 818 feet, some atop Streeter's dumping like the game of hand-over-hand.[30]

Once the Cap'n knew the mighty were reluctant to file a major challenge against him, he loved irritating them. Ma hung her wash on a line outside the house/scow, and the friendly couple invited the homeless to share their quarters. Perhaps his shabby guests helped Streeter pull weeds, find firewood and repair his makeshift house. But not everyone was welcome. Sometime in 1890, the Cap'n wounded a Samuel Avery as the man was trying to erect a boathouse on vacant land after asking Fairbank's permission. Avery received his red badge of courage in retreat and was not seriously hurt, since the shotgun was probably loaded with just birdshot, tiny pellets that are not fatal to humans. We have no account of the trial, but the Cap'n presumably was acquitted on the grounds that he had been defending his property. This was the only time Streeter is known to have shot someone, not even in the 1902 gunfight that landed him in prison.[31]

The state finally authorized construction of the nearly completed Lake Shore Drive in 1889, legalizing what had been going on for three years. But further work was delayed because several owners of small holdings were fed up with the city and state's failure to put up a seawall by their land. They held off ceding riparian rights for property that was or was often underwater unless the Drive was built half a mile farther into the lake. They first discussed the issue in January 1892 with representatives of Fairbank, Farwell, Walter Newberry, former mayor De Witt Cregier Sr. and trustees of the Newberry estate, which had given the city a major research library. Negotiators for the two sides held sixty-six meetings (!) until everyone was satisfied with a compromise that you can still see, since the Drive swings out at a lakeward angle from Bellevue to Ohio Street.[32]

Other small property owners proved just as difficult. With Palmer's preference for using stand-ins unconnected with the city, he had attorney Henry Cooper of suburban LaGrange pose as an individual speculator interested in shoreland lots. Cooper talked former park commission president Ezra Butler into selling one at Oak and Pine for what was a fortune then, $90,000. At the time, reclaimed land that had not yet been smoothed out for the Drive or its feeder streets stayed as lumpy as a tray of kitty litter, and the Cap'n did nothing to make it prettier.

Ohio Street near the lake in 1915. Streeter's persistence kept this area undeveloped until after his eviction in the year this photo was taken. *Chicago History Museum.*

Moving a bit back in time, Fairbank had said in a letter to a newspaper that his clashes with the Cap'n would be "a comedy" if it were not for the possibility that someone might be hurt. On May 7, 1890, authorities set several wooden structures on Streeter's claim on fire—yet not the Streeters' home/scow. We lack details and must assume they destroyed the shacks of other squatters, instead, and perhaps two small boats the Cap'n had been repairing. On September 9, Fairbank won an eviction suit, but Streeter stayed put and insisted he was waiting for the Illinois Supreme Court to order him off. As usual, he was all talk. He and Maria moved off but then came back, and a justice of the peace let him stay.

Disgruntled Fairbank took the case one step higher, to Cook County Circuit Court. On Friday, November 6, 1891, a judge rendered a decision in Streeter's favor, but it was not to be promulgated—made public—until the following Monday. John V. Farwell's son Arthur was so sure the decision was against Streeter that on Saturday he along with an agent for his father, named Auger, and two policemen tore down a fence the Cap'n had used to mark his claim.

Streeter came over and picked up part of the fallen fence, but one of the officers knocked it from his hand. They then found a revolver in his pocket and booked him for carrying a concealed weapon. John V. arrived and ordered Auger to level a squatter's hut and cart away the furniture, but Streeter's home/scow and possessions were left untouched. The millionaires seemed to be giving the Cap'n special treatment at a time when interlopers were dealt with harshly. Sometime earlier, the park commission got rid of a private pier by dynamiting it at two o'clock in the morning. Anyway, Arthur Farwell's workers put up a three-sided fence, with the lake as the fourth side, that encompassed less than Streeter had staked out for himself. The Cap'n swore out warrants against Arthur, Auger and both officers, but nothing came of it. Taking another approach, Fairbank took his complaints to Cook County Superior Court, but the Cap'n's lawyer scored a victory by claiming Fairbank's riparian rights covered only natural accretion and not landfill, and so keeping a homestead there was permissible.[33]

With no one offering him money to leave, Streeter needed a source of income, if only to keep himself in cigars. Hoping the U.S. Army would overlook his desertion, he applied twice for a disability pension, giving his address as "the Foot of Superior Street, Chicago, Ill." Both requests were rejected, and one reply noted that he still owed the government his Henry rifle. Impatient to feel successful, the Cap'n was selling off lots in June 1891, and the shore owners still left him alone. General Land Office recorder Chester Brush snidely asserted that most purchasers were servant girls and laborers, though at least one owned a small business. A few buyers applied for building permits but were turned down.

As Streeter fended off attempts to remove him, Lake Shore Drive was so attractive a residential district that it was upending the city's concentration of wealth. We know that the John Gates home at 2944 South Michigan, which had cost $300,000 a few decades earlier, was sold for just $65,500 in 1908. Over the years, other mansions along once-prestigious South Michigan Avenue near 18th Street could be purchased so cheaply that construction of large stone houses virtually ceased except for on the Drive and its side streets. In contrast, the value for a section near Palmer's castle rose from $160 a front foot in 1882, just after Potter conceived of the district, to $800 in 1892, and before long would reach $1,500 and keep rising.[34]

In late 1891, Streeter shook hands with Alderman Edward Cullerton over some lots at future East Walton Place. The councilman, half-hidden by a huge mustache and a short beard over his plump face, even hired muscular young mechanic William McManners as a guard not only for this portion but also the rest of Streeterville. The Cap'n apparently sold lots and greeted visitors during the day and then walked over to his side job in the evening. Edward O. Brown said the conniver operated a nighttime restaurant in an abandoned trolley on a downtown vacant lot at South Michigan and Adams Street and threatened to sue anyone trying to move him off. A contractor about to put up a building there "suffered Mr. Streeter to blackmail them to the extent of several hundred dollars," said Brown.

The Cap'n had made himself such a character that by 1892 the community name of "Streeterville" had stuck.[35] With cash from the buyoff and unknown amounts from selling lots owned by Fairbank and Farwell, he purchased a brick eight-flat at 74th and Vincennes Avenue and ran a grocery on the ground floor. In this cloudy period in his life, it is possible that, to maintain ownership of the one-time marsh, he left Maria to face constables in the converted scow while he sold salt and ketchup to housewives and workmen from South Side factories. Prosecutors in his first murder trial charged that in the early 1890s, Streeter also claimed land he did not own at the shore of Wolf Lake, shared with Indiana.

The Cap'n must have enjoyed spinning legends to enshrine himself as a real-life American folk hero like Johnny Appleseed and Casey Jones. He said that one morning, seeing police captain Michael Schaak and a patrolman coming near his home/scow, he slipped out with his shotgun and leaped at them. He alleged that he "delivered a knockout blow on the head and shoulders of Schaak, who dropped like a log," and the patrolman ran off. This was mild compared to his outrageous stories. There is a pattern to all of Streeter's tales. When he said, "It was in all the papers," the story is told with a wink, but the others always have some truth in them.

6

George Wellington Streeter was merely one claimant to the uneven shore, but most of the others sought to profit from commercial lake traffic rather than residences. Chicago's 1892 shipping season saw nearly twenty-two thousand boat or ship arrivals and departures, said to have been more than Philadelphia, New York City and Boston combined. Many of the vessels carried Michigan lumber to build churches and whorehouses in the West.

Disputes over the shore began in 1836, when the end of the Blackhawk Indian war forced Native Americans to sign a treaty and move out. To raise funds for a barge canal connecting the Illinois River with Lake Michigan, the state sent William Thornton, William Archer and future Chicago mayor Gurdon Hubbard to sell unsettled areas. They could have unloaded the city's neglected shore but instead urged that the strand be left "open, clear and free of any buildings or other obstructions whatever." Though not binding, their advice established guidelines that continue in effect.

Storm-driven breakers and the downward scoop of currents wiped away much of the downtown shore and threatened to destroy South Michigan Avenue, the city's grand boulevard before Lake Shore Drive. In 1869, the Illinois Central Railroad received state authorization to fill in the shore from 12th Street (Roosevelt Road) to Randolph Street so that its trains could travel directly from the South Side to warehouses along the river, a decision that would become crucial in the modern Near North Side. Meanwhile, the city made up for erosion by dumping rubble from the 1871 fire off what became

Grant Park. The railroad continued dumping for land creation beyond its needs until the U.S. Supreme Court ordered it to stop because it was interfering with city plans for what became Monroe Harbor.[36]

There was still no end to misuses of the shore. Chicago's chain of beaches owes its existence largely to eyesores that mail order magnate A. Montgomery Ward saw from his office window on South Michigan: a deteriorating glass exhibition hall, the ugly Illinois Central tracks and train sheds and a U.S. Army garbage incinerator. Around these were freight wagons, garbage heaps and a few squatter shacks. Disgusted, he began a twenty-year, $50,000 fight to file suits against the city and private interests for violating the dictum about keeping the lakefront free for the public. Ward became the most hated and misunderstood man in Chicago. He won nearly every civil action but was unable to stop the city from using the foot of Randolph Street for dumping manure and other sweepings from the Loop. His efforts led to a landscaped Grant Park downtown. "Had I known in 1890 how long it would take me to preserve a park for the people against their will," Ward said as he wore out, "I doubt if I would have taken it."[37]

Architect Daniel Burnham had earlier proposed ideas for improving much of the city's twenty miles of shore. "The lake has been singing to us many years until we have been responsive," said the man reported to have urged, "Make no little plans, they have no power to stir men's souls." The Commercial Club of Chicago invited Burnham to elaborate on his idea, and he stressed in his 1909 Plan of Chicago that "the Lakefront by right belongs to the people." He evidently was inspired by Lake Shore Drive to sketch out an "Outer Park Boulevard" along the rim of downtown. A generation later, the two grand thoroughfares would be joined.

When the shipping season ended in the late autumn of 1893, a national recession made temporary work hard to find. Tugboat captain Charles Williams dug through eleven feet of mushy sandland off Erie Street until he reached clay, then used boards to fashion a one-room, sit-down home for the winter. The roof was covered with a layer of soil. In time, two other squatters came to live with him. Since Williams said they would move out when the shipping season resumed, police let them alone.

Peter Johnson, a former boat captain from Ireland, moved into a "cave" (deep hole) some boys had hollowed out and stayed put as the sand and silt grew around him. In 1878, he bought an old bathhouse 300 feet off Indiana Street (Grand Avenue) and in time used it to sell liquor for men coming in from a nearby lumber yard. Since the city ignored his complaints about the Ogden dock company's dumping around the bathhouse, he fenced in 150 by 250 feet of landfill lying on top his accretion and claimed it as his own. Johnson might have lived out his life there but was somehow encouraged to move on for construction of Lake Shore Drive, and the General Land Office ruled against his claim in 1896.

A scatterbrain named William Cox reasoned that the lake really belonged to the Indians. The St. Joseph River Pottawatomies of Michigan were descended from people who had lived where the city now stands. The tribal trustee in Dowagiac, Michigan, was willing to take a small sum for a worthless deed, helping Cox's claim for a four-hundred-mile track from 39th Street through the north shore and up to Lake Superior. A Chicago Board of Trade broker in cahoots with Cox in January 1902 paid more than three hundred claimants $100 each for their supposed birthright. But the federal government ruled that Indians had relinquished any hold to the shore with a treaty in the 1830s.[38]

A more serious challenge to the shore owners came from the McKee scrip holders. In 1896, speculators Mathias Benner and Harvey LaFollette obtained a document Congress had issued forty-three years earlier to the children of William McKee, a soldier in the Mexican-American War. The scrippers said this entitled them to 160 acres of any vacant land of their choosing, and they chose Streeterville. The scrippers sent a representative to John V. Farwell and probably other shore owners requesting an unknown sum to keep from pressing their claim. Rebuffed, they plotted to jump in immediately after William McKinley was sworn in as president in the hope that he might sign anything without looking into its legitimacy or likely consequences. Treasury Secretary John Carlisle was induced with a $20,000 retainer to provide them with legal advice the second he left office, but their hastiness aroused suspicion and the matter was put off. A newspaper said the case "began to get unpleasantly notorious."[39]

Fairbank filed a protest that led to one legal action after another until November 23, 1896, when corrupt General Land Office commissioner Silas Lamoreaux conducted a sham hearing in the nation's capital. Bogus evidence included "an affidavit of a venerable [elderly] negro, or halfbreed, to the effect that he remembered [early resident] Robert A. McKinzie, somewhere about 1837, in a Chicago barber shop remark to two other persons that he did not claim any land east of Sand Street," Brown said. After a flurry of telegrams between Brown and federal officials, Lamoreaux resigned and was instantly hired at the scrippers' law office. A new land office commissioner reaffirmed that the state had properly sold the land, leaving a number of speculators in the United Kingdom and France holding worthless pieces of paper.[40]

Sometime around late 1894, nine Streeter supporters presented to the General Land Office in Washington an 1812 military boundary warrant and applied for Plat A, the entire Lake Shore Drive area. Not only was the claim rejected on its own grounds, but the warrant had also previously been used to locate land out West. Brown said "Streeter, or someone acting for him, had got hold of it, erased the old location and attempted to pass it as an unused warrant." No charges were filed.

Sheldon & Ogden, the real estate division of the Chicago Canal & Dock Company, used the lengthy Lake Shore Drive reclamation project as a cover for extensive land-creation dumping at Oak and Indiana Streets (Grand Avenue) as a replacement for its pier. This new land was off former marsh lots owned by the McCormick and Ogden estates. After Illinois attorney general Moloney lost a suit challenging the action, the dock company sliced through its landfill for a short "canal" or inlet eighteen feet deep and then leased both sides to warehouse owners and the Cudahy Meat Packing company. A companion but narrower inlet was dug near the first and was eventually filled in.

The new land jutting into the lake came to be called the Ogden Slip and served as a harbor for wooden ships with such cargoes as molasses and sugar from the Gulf Coast and Caribbean as the city grew into a food manufacturing center. The Illinois Supreme Court's 1896 decision that the state owned the shore stopped all unauthorized private dumping for land creation, but lawmakers still had questions about the legality of the Ogden Slip. General Fitz-Simons testified at a hearing that the dredging and dumping had brought some of the expanded shore slope—called its "face"—into navigable waters. The company defended its slicing through the new land to accommodate shops by saying riparian rights defined what an owner could add to the shore but not what he might take away from it. Unpersuaded, the Illinois House commission issued a biting 1911 report stating that "what was pretended originally to be a great public harbor enterprise, merely became a cloak of one of the greatest land grabs (considering its value) recorded in modern history."[41]

7

The routine of fighting off constables and city agents was not grand enough for Streeter. Speaking at length to his lawyer friend Francis X. Busch, he embellished what must have been a common raid into an epic. The Cap'n said he fired birdshot at one hundred men marching across his land. Most of them fled, but "there were 33 of them that didn't get up." He claimed he piled a dozen of the wounded into a garbage wagon and transported them to a police station so he could have them charged with disorderly conduct. He added that the newspapers termed conditions "a state of anarchy," but "nuthin' happened."

Besides being naturally friendly, Streeter may have made daily rounds downtown since he never knew who might become a buyer. In addition, he always took care of "down and outers," as Busch said. The Cap'n usually found them by the river docks or around Clark Street saloons. He gave them a meal or let them stay in one of the empty shacks. We can't say how many huts there were or who built them, but an 1891 Rascher fire insurance map gives seven little boxes. There could have been more. Busch said a couple of years later that perhaps two dozen people down on their luck were "more or less permanent residents." That didn't last. On some pretext, city crews arrived in force on September 20, 1901, dismantled several shacks and piled the wood into wagons for dumping off Randolph Street. Not long afterward, Streeter was seen selling lots again on the millionaires' district.[42]

Eviction writ in hand, Fairbank organized a D-Day push to remove the Cap'n and Maria for good on February 8, 1893. At 10:00 a.m., Chief

Constable Frank Putnam led what a newspaper called one hundred carpenters, wagon drivers and sheriff's deputies. They forced their way inside the house/scow and flung out furniture and personal possessions, including an iron stove still hot. As Maria went downtown to fetch her husband, the hired men pushed a small piano down to the pile of goods and the carpenters nailed together sections of a plank fence to close off the claim. Other men put jackscrews under the former boat to install skids, leaving the uninhabitable *Reutan* alone.

Returning, Maria and the Cap'n saw men dismantling their home. Streeter pretended to be beaten, but his mind was clicking away. This rare instance of a documented confrontation has all the drama of the Cap'n's fabrications. He waited until his long guns were added to the pile, then surreptitiously slid them under a carpet. Carpenters ignored the couple as teamed horses tugged the scow off its three-foot mound. "You're the hired tools of rich men," Streeter shouted, gun in hand. By the time Fairbank's attorney could return with a warrant, the middle-aged squatter had taken up a position inside the ruin. The shouting and threats continued until sensible police captain Barny Baer persuaded Streeter to calm down and surrender. Released on bond, Streeter knocked down a citizen told to guard the land and fired potshots at three constables inside the scow. Maria was so upset after contacting a lawyer named Thompson that she visited a gin mill. As she left, she attacked a police officer and was charged with disorderly conduct.

After dragging the partially dismantled scow onto a street, workmen replaced boundary fence sections that Streeter and his people had torn down. The desolate *Reutan*, now named the *Maria*, was abandoned on Lake Shore Drive.[43] A reporter later found Maria and attorney Thompson on a small boat called the *Cautious Clara*, perhaps one of the vessels the Cap'n had been patching up. The lawyer reported that Streeter was selling lots for $250 to $500 per front foot. Maria put in that "when the Cap has sold a little more of the ground we may take a notion to build [on it]; and, if we do, it will be something…which will take the shine off Palmer's castle."

The Streeters met another setback when Circuit Court Judge William Ewing dismissed their complaint against Fairbank. Waffling, Ewing held that Streeter's motion had no legal standing because he had let his attorney sign it for him. The questionable finding took away the Streeters' home and their livelihood: lot selling. Streeter was so low on funds that he arranged to pay court costs by installment.[44]

Although crews had graded all that remained of the undeveloped former marsh, Fairbank and the other owners refrained from lucrative subleasing.

"District of Lake Michigan" map printed for William Niles, self-proclaimed military governor of the independent federal district. *Chicago History Museum.*

Evidently, the Palmer circle had been watching trends and talking to buyers, waiting for the right time before leasing their lots for development. But a photo of the no-man's land from around this time shows seven brownstone apartment buildings on Farwell's property between Superior and Chicago Avenue, all three stories tall. Either John V. had received permission from Palmer for this or had broken the pact.

The Cap'n somehow became involved with several shady men calling themselves the North American Deposit & Investment Company. Its main activity in 1893–94 was sectioning off Streeter's claim into twenty-five lots, then selling and buying, and reselling and rebuying the same lots among themselves to drive up the value on paper. The investment company told anyone interested that all firmament not indicated in the faulty John Wall survey of 1821 was "found land" created by Streeter and resulting accretion and that this constituted the (U.S.) District of Lake Michigan. The Cap'n said, "If the city wants to annex us and treat us half-way decent we stand ready to come in." He boasted of selling more than forty lots "to good, respectable persons, and I don't take less than $10,000 a lot for them."

This was too much. Newspapers set out to prove that the colorful character was nothing but a criminal, noting that the frequency of title transfers suggested fraud. County Recorder Samuel Chase asked the state's attorney's office for an indictment, but nothing was done, the latest inaction keeping the legality of Lake Shore Drive property out of the upper courts.[45]

With money from selling bogus lots, the Cap'n stocked his grocery at 7351 South Vincennes Avenue. When Deputy C.J. Jones showed up to talk about missing payments on court costs on March 11, 1894, a Saturday, the Streeters gave him a meal and chased him out with a shotgun. The couple next had two friends help them barricade the grocery for a siege. After a quiet weekend, sheriff's police surrounded the shop on Monday, and a newspaper claimed, the Cap'n called out for them to "seek a warmer climate" while pointing his shotgun at the door. Using a battering ram of two-by-fours, the officers broke in and overpowered him. But he apparently justified his actions to a judge and was let go to peddle lots he did not own again.[46] Since there is no further mention of the South Side grocery, perhaps he sold it at this time.

With newspapers showing the Cap'n as a fraud, he needed an official-looking document to "prove" his claim. Sometime in 1894, one of his friends, probably William Cox, seems to have helped him work out the details. The certificate reads:

Now know ye that the United States of America in consideration of the premises and in conformity of several Acts of Congress in such cases and provided have given and granted by these presents do give and grant to George Wellington Streeter and his heirs the said tract above described, to have and to hold forever. In testimony whereby I, Grover Cleveland, President of the United States of America, have caused these letters to be made patent and the seal of the General Land Office to be hereunto fixed. Given under my hand at the City of Washington on March 19, 1895. [Signed] Grover Cleveland, president; Hoke Smith, Secretary of the Land Office; Silas Wright Lamoreaux, Recorder in the General Land Office.

For one thing, the patent never existed, and Lamoreaux was commissioner at the time rather than recorder. Smith was secretary of the interior, not the person to sign patents, and his first name was Oake, not Hoke. In addition, the only patent Cleveland signed was for a friend. Edward O. Brown said that Streeter or his accomplice must have obtained a copy of an old patent, chemically removed portions and substituted the names of officials.[47]

Lake Shore Drive grew by a small piece of land at Chicago Avenue that the city had been reserving for a possible new structure in its waterworks complex. After a judge mentioned that the unused strip should be turned into parkland, the city transferred its title to the Lincoln Park Commission in 1895. A member believed the agency then entered into an arrangement with private persons to build "a proposed drive," actually furthering Lake Shore Drive. The unnamed "private persons" proceeded to fill in about fifty feet, but the transaction was not made public for two years.[48]

A sinister character now snaked about Streeter's life: attorney Henry N. Cooper, a former agent for Potter Palmer and currently secretary of the Pine Street Land Association. He also headed an out-of-town investors group called the North Shore Association. As part of his duties, Cooper kept track of every possibly illegal thing Streeter was doing, and evidently he was the one who had supplied authorities with a copy of the forged Cleveland patent. Lacking guile, the Cap'n failed to pick up hints that someone was out to trap him.

No prompt action was taken about the bogus patent, although Lake Shore Drive was filling up with some of the city's best citizens. By 1898, residents included A.B. Dick, president of the mimeograph firm, at no. 21; lumber tycoon John Loomis at 55; Robert Todd Lincoln at 60; independent minister David Swing of Central Church at 66; esteemed attorney Franklin MacVeagh at 111; Mahlon Ogden's widow at 117; Barbara Armour, widow of meatpacker George Armour, at 120; George Armour Capet, of the same family, at 125; A.C. McClurg, of the McClurg printing company, at 125; and Orrin Potter, vice president of the Commercial National Bank, at 130, all in the original numbering.

Yet mansions like these were falling out of favor, as foreseen in the second phase of Palmer's grand scheme. In 1903, a luxury apartment building was allowed to be erected at 23 Lake Shore Drive. This was not far from Ogden McClurg's home at 125, but by 1913, McClurg had sold the mansion and moved to the large Marshall Apartments, at 999 Lake Shore Drive in the original numbering. Many of the Marshall's tenants had "receiving Monday" after their names. In 1916, Medill McCormick left his mansion and moved to a large apartment building at 936, and other new vertical residences were constructed at 950, 199, 106, 1100, 1130, 1150, 120 (the Stewart Apartments), 1220 and 1240, all in the original numbering. These do not include exclusive high-rises built on streets leading to the Drive. By then, the paved Drive extension stretched from Indiana Street (Grand Avenue) to past Cedar Street, and the general public could tell it was not welcomed. However, the road was graced by a bicycle path and a beach forty-eight feet wide, paved with slippery granite blocks rather than sand.

Streeter's encampment was not only at the front door of mansion row, but it also lay close enough to a hobo district to be considered one and the same in the minds of society. The area known as "Fishtown" sprang up around 1899 in a neglected patch by Hubbard and the Pine Street excursion boat dock. One might find fifty to two hundred tramps around shacks made from rough wooden pallets taken from the nearby A. Booth fish packing company, giving the area its nickname. No one attempted to break up the hobo village because tramps were useful for providing election roll names, multiple voting and doing odd jobs for a quarter. Judging from their monikers and accents, the shabby residents came from as far as "Frisco" and London.[49]

In time, the hobo district gave way to respectability, and we no longer hear of the fallacious investment company—perhaps its members dissolved rather than face charges. Left on his own, Streeter made a last attempt to legalize his bogus claim. He submitted a "homestead entry" with the secretary of the interior, but it was rejected on the ground that the U.S. government had no jurisdiction over the shore. From now on, whatever happened would be pure bluff, as stakes kept rising in the form of property values.

The Drive was so amazing that the *Chicago Times* campaigned to extend it all the way to the South Side, possibly by turning the city's edge into a succession of beaches that would absorb angry waves. But the Drive was not yet finished. Working with the North Township Board, representing residents in what was about to become part of the North Side, attorney Cooper persuaded the final holdouts, the Allmendinger family, to let the Drive be built across their land. To do this, he posed as the agent of an investment syndicate owning below-water lots north of Pearson Street. More significantly, Cooper also hired guards to keep watch on Streeter. They were probably no better trained or disciplined than the "private detectives" the Cap'n was hiring.

8

The undisturbed Streeter encampment had become a squatter village of shacks and tents. From unclear accounts, it seems that sixteen people, including his watchmen, were permanent dwellers and twelve others regularly came by from their homes in the city or steady jobs. The mixture of the homeless and the shopkeeping class nailed together a few prefabricated, single-story "government buildings" to make the District of Lake Michigan a reality with an uncertain future.

Evidently, eccentrics have a magnetic force that draws other eccentrics to them, such as Streeter's rapport with William Cox and now William Niles, a slender, nice-looking man in his twenties with a full mustache and wavy hair. We first hear of him as he pumped the squatter king up with a scheme for permanently possessing the land by force. Niles might just have been enchanted by impossible causes. With the Cap'n's sense of humor and grandness, he agreed to secede from Illinois.

On April 5, 1899, residents of the encampment voted to accept the flag and Constitution of the United States as theirs. Nearly three weeks later, Streeter appointed himself territorial governor and was elected district clerk. All able-bodied men except those in higher office were handed deputy marshal badges, one imagines from a five-and-dime. Under Military Governor Niles, men served this notice at the homes or offices of Mayor Carter Harrison II, Chief of Police Joseph Kipley and corporation counsel Charles Walker: "All persons unlawfully occupying the land of the District of Lake Michigan would be considered trespassers after the 1st Day of May, 1899."

Streeter joshed with reporters that the district treasury held $159,000 to fight off challenges and erect more public buildings in addition to a giant tower that would overshadow Eiffel's. Three men went to Farwell's mansion at 109 Pearson to serve notice that he must eject his tenants from his apartment buildings by the end of the month. Farwell told the leader to write "U.S." in front of his district title, which would make this a criminal misrepresentation. The man dithered and tore up the notice.

The May 1 deadline passed uneventfully. Dawn the next morning saw a city hall conference involving North Side inspector Max Heidelmeier; acting mayor Walker; and, as a representative of the shore owners, Fairbank's son Kellogg. He was a thirty-year-old lawyer active in civic affairs. First assistant corporation counsel Browning contended that authorities had no legal grounds for destroying the district, since the courts had not ruled against the squatters and they were not causing trouble. But acting police chief Lewis grew impatient with all the crisscrossing opinions and ordered preparations for an invasion.[50]

At daylight on Thursday, May 4, twenty-eight men of the district piled reinforcing dirt against boards they had erected around their claim, and then an odd assortment of pipe-dreamers raised an American flag up a pole nailed to the makeshift courthouse. Since there is no mention of Maria or the wife of Streeter guard Billy McManners, the Cap'n might have gallantly had the women stay away to keep them from harm. A rumor said downtown shops had refused to sell him any weapons.

To justify their stand, Niles, with his scrambled intelligence, came up with:

DECLARATION OF THE DISTRICT OF LAKE MICHIGAN

To Whom it May Concern:

Greetings—

When in the course of human events, it becomes necessary for any body of men to take up arms in defence of their property and legal rights, a cause must exist....

And, whereas, cities and states do not grow by annexation, and as there are no records to show that the City of Chicago or State of Illinois, ever annexed any of the territory east of the United States survey of 1821 known as the meandering line;

And whereas police authority does not exist beyond its Municipal boundaries, the fact must remain, that all of the 100 or more arrests made by the police of the city of Chicago in the District of Lake Michigan [clearly an multiplication] *have been unlawful and were made with malicious intent either for hire or personal malice;...*

And whereas, Capt. Streeter lived in his wrecked steamer several years, and the land formed around it until it connected with the main land, he was then ordered by certain very wealthy men, who live on the shore that he must leave, [was] told that their land grew, that they had riparian rights, and that he could not law with them. Hundreds of arrests followed, but no convictions were ever made.[51]

When John V. Farwell, good-looking Kellogg Fairbank and Newberry Library president Fishburn came over to make Streeter listen to reason, the balding holdover from pioneer days merely showed them an old map marking St. Clair Street as the city's eastern boundary. Police gave him a day to enjoy his fantasy of independence. Then dozens of people filled the streets after midnight to watch the clash. In the early morning dark of May 5, the first wagonload of officers from a number of districts pulled up to the East Chicago Avenue station as a deployment site. The stage was set for drama, but spectators witnessed a comedy

Diminutive Deputy U.S. Marshal Patterson stepped over the line dividing the district from Illinois but was stopped by two of the Cap'n's guards, then several nesters weakened his resolve by flashing their tin stars. Patterson said it looked like rain and he must be going. Streeter was sitting with some of his people on a small rise when at 10:30 a.m. Inspector Heidelmeier and Captain John L. Revere led a swarm of bluecoats, possibly wearing tall riot helmets. Streeter returned to his newspaper but then cried out to his supporters, "We're here to stay!" Around him were about thirty-five believers, some with weapons tucked behind their belts.

Beefy Max Heidelmeier laughed when a sentry told him he could not enter and took down a bar across the gate himself. Next, the inspector—that is, a captain entrusted with a large section of the city—brandished his nightstick while ordering all to disperse. From his wood chair, Streeter reasserted his ownership and supposedly asked, "Do you know what them fellows [mansion dwellers] claim? They claim riparian rights, that's what they claim. What is riparian rights? Riparian rights is the right to repair yer shore when it's wore off by water." Unamused, the Bavarian grabbed him by the collar of his frock coat and started him in a rush toward a patrol wagon. Not a shot had been fired.

The police grabbed about fifteen supporters while the rest scattered. The possibly hundreds of spectators—one account claims there were one thousand—jeered as the prisoners entered paddy wagons. Niles apparently caused trouble and was beaten as his wagon headed for the station.

Everyone was charged with unlawful assembly, with a possible fine of one hundred dollars. Why not trespassing, assault (threatening force), unlawful assembly, impersonating federal agents or resisting arrest? The reason may be that Streeter had no friends among the police or prosecutors, but the shore owners did.[52]

Possibly irked at the light charges, a judge improperly set their bail at five times higher than what their fines could be. In the basement lockup, skinny Streeter assured reporters that all necessary papers for acknowledging the district as a separate government were on file in Washington: "We're only waiting for an act of Congress, and it'll be rushed in the next session." A little after noon, he sent out for lunch for his followers and had the food served behind bars. The meal brought the district treasury down to $112.79.

Farwell told a newspaper he was providing his watchmen with guns, since Chicago officers at the time were issued firearms only in dangerous situations. John V. informed his people that the weapons would be, in his tangled syntax, "to protect yourself, and any forcible entry by anybody without process of law makes such transgression, liable to be shot as a mad dog if they do not on your orders desist from such attempts." The *Chicago Tribune* concurred, editorializing that "the farce playing out at the foot of Superior Street has been going on too long."[53]

The Cap'n may have joked and tall-taled like his old self, but a curious sense of seriousness and even nobleness was seeping into his personality, as seen in subsequent events. This was a case where a chronic liar comes to believe his lies, and Farwell's "shoot as a mad dog" letter to the *Tribune* may have been the start. Streeter would bitterly refer to that phrase repeatedly over the years.

Fairbank notified the police that, in effect, if *you* don't do anything *we* will. On Monday afternoon, May 7, a sergeant and eight officers stood by as men hired by Farwell and the Newberry estate tore everything apart and torched the pile. Recalling the ruins of Carthage, a newspaper said, "Not only the capital itself but all of Streeterville was destroyed, and not one shingle was permitted to rest upon another." The criminal charges against the Cap'n and his supporters seem to have been intentionally forgotten.

9

Wealthy residents must have thought there was no way Streeter would return, but they were unaware of William Niles. Still acting as military governor, he convinced several Streeter supporters in January 1900 that they could retake the district by attacking its one unprotected boundary: the lake. They voted a five-dollar levy per man to finance the action and hire lawyers, and Niles issued one of his proclamations: "All lots upon which the taxes have not been paid, except those exempt from taxation [the Water Tower waterworks], are hereby declared to be the property of the Government of the District of Lake Michigan."

On May 25, Niles walked to the harbor at the mouth of the river and handed a naval captain an open letter to President McKinley about protecting the district's sovereignty. The next night, thirteen defenders boarded a pair of small boats on the Calumet River at 66th Street. The Streeterville navy sailed under several bridges to the lake, then north just past the Chicago River. At 2:00 a.m. on Saturday, May 27, residents near Superior heard the greatest racket ever made on the North Side, a Gatling gun cranked as a warning for everyone to stay away. The second boat then sailed back with the contraption. Patrolman James O'Malley was ready to arrest the crew that had just anchored, but his watch commander told him by phone to await reinforcements. The defenders splashed through shallow water and hoisted an American flag, which Niles believed made the district a lawful U.S. possession, like the Philippines.[54]

The defenders dug a "bombproof" on each side of Superior just off the shore. The shallow bunkers were about twelve feet square and roofed over with some sort of covering and rocks. Niles called them "forts." The six-foot leader marked off what he believed he and his men could hold; then they waited. Early morning amblers were startled to see someone poking a rifle at them. Lincoln Park secretary George Erby tried to gallop his buggy through the enemy lines, but the defenders fired a warning and grabbed his reins. Niles splintered the carriage of former police captain Barney Baer, now head of the park police and wounded his horse. A deliveryman giving his daughter a ride was "prodded" with a sentry's rifle, and a bullet fired at the police wounded a fourteen-year-old boy standing among the spectators.

The strategy worked out was for Chief Kipley to lead the right flank while Baer charged with the left. Six patrol wagons were hurriedly equipped with rifles, and four hundred officers (!) were sent to the Chicago Avenue waterworks as a reserve. Fifteen bluecoats hopped aboard a leased steam tug and lugged with them a couple of three-inch field guns from the nearby national guard armory. This was overkill for Lincoln Park policeman William Hayes. He approached Niles's men by himself and said, "Say, fellers, cut it out." He and a park official then talked Niles into surrendering on the promise that he would not be hurt. But the military governor refused to relinquish his rifle and was "pounded up severely" in front of onlookers, a newspaper said.

The thwarted defenders were charged with offenses ranging from unlawful assembly to assault with intent to kill, and bail was set at $6,000 per man. The Cap'n had not been present for the confrontation but appeared at the station later. He said of Niles's beating that "nothing of the sort would be allowed in any city of the United States except Chicago." With no bail money left in the district treasury, half a dozen supporters remained in jail for four months before they were acquitted, guilty though they were.

For a while after that, no one seemed to know where the Cap'n and Maria had gone, maybe Indiana. Wherever he went, later events suggest that Streeter was worried he might lose his claim to the millionaire district unless he returned to it. He opened an office in Parlor H of Chicago's Tremont Hotel and told a reporter, "Ours is the only democratic government ever formed on the face of the earth. It is ruled by the sovereign of the sand."

On September 1, 1901, Streeter and about fifteen lot buyers set up tents off Pearson on property owned by Louisa Healy. Police declined to interfere "as long as they behave themselves." The strong-willed widow of famed portrait painter G.P.A. Healy demanded action, and on September

20, Captain Revere served notice that all squatters must vacate in six hours or face arrest. Streeter sadly joked with the police as workmen tore apart a partially built courthouse and district council chambers. Streeter guard Billy McManners drew a revolver when officers tried to force him out, but Barney Baer overpowered him as the Cap'n's small dog jumped into the fight. Afterward, Streeter rode in one of the wagons hauling the ruins to the end of Randolph Street.[55]

No one doubted that he was planning a return. A few days after the eviction, he swore in twenty men as deputy marshals, actually bodyguards and watchmen, without mentioning that he could not pay them. On October 5, 1901, the Cap'n pretended to be abandoning his claim as he drove out of the unofficial dump with his guards in the back of the wagon, followed by McManners in the seat of a mule-drawn wagon carrying the reclaimed lumber. After crossing the small Rush Street bridge, the two wagons made a sharp turn to the forbidden land in full view of the surprised police and the cheers of supporters.[56]

10

N.K. Fairbank had said there was a possibility that someone might be hurt in the clashes with Streeter, and now that seemed inevitable. With her English resolve, Louisa Healy conferred with a former park commission president and possibly shadowy attorney Henry Cooper about ways of keeping the bewhiskered squatter in jail. This was at a time when Streeter's unpaid guards walked off, leaving just the Cap'n and Maria living in their wagon with tenting over it, and Billy McManners staying with his wife and young child in a wooden hut paid for by Alderman Cullerton. The walkout so upset Maria that she sought solace at a Clark Street saloon, was turned away and kicked in all the street-level windows. She was booked at the Central District station. Even the congenial Cap'n turned snappish. On October 21, 1901, he attacked attorney Arthur Wells with a club or gun butt as the man tried to serve an injunction from Louisa Healy.[57]

Cullerton used his city influence to obtain a building permit so that the Cap'n and Maria might stay out of trouble by having a home and a small store off Chestnut Street. Lacking a foundation, the long, single-story brick building facing the mansions was not considered a permanent structure. Some homeless people built shacks near it, arousing such concern that U.S. General Land Office recorder Chester Brush arrived from Washington to tell a Cook County grand jury that the Cleveland patent was "a clumsy forgery." He also denounced as fakes all the signatures on Streeter's abstracts and titles. On January 31, 1902, the Cap'n was indicted on fraud charges for selling lots for whatever he could get. This was the first time he had been charged with a felony, and being acquitted would not be as simple as talking his way out in a justice of the peace court. Bail was set at $1,000.[58]

Drifter Henry "Klondike" Hoeldtke came to live in McManners's little pine house as a watchman. Also staying there was William Force, whom the Cap'n had hired as a guard in August on the promise of two dollars a day. At the same time, attorney Henry Cooper was known to visit the "cabins" of two nearby shore owner guards, named Dugan and Henry Russer, even though a Judge Chamberlain had enjoined him and his assistants from putting foot on the disputed land. With Streeter hiring guards, the shore owners hired several more. One of them was young John Kirk from bandit-plagued Missouri.[59]

Violence was in the air as Cooper went to the East Chicago Avenue station on February 22, 1902, and asked Patrolman James O'Malley to accompany him "as a matter of protection" on a walk to the wasteland, as a newspaper put it. His purpose is unknown. Seeing them approaching, McManners and Hoeldtke stepped out of Billy's hut with rifles and stealthily moved through the weeds in the early dark. Holding a rifle or shotgun, Streeter came from his wagon-tent and shouted at the intruders, "You've got no business here!" because of the judge's ruling. McManners and Hoeldtke prodded them with rifles and told them to start walking backward with their hands up. Streeter knocked Cooper down with his rifle butt; then the lawyer rose and walked butt-first for nearly two blocks to Pine Street, renamed Lincoln Park Boulevard, probably to acknowledge the western border of the Gold Coast created by the drive.

What happened next is unclear. The Cap'n said he returned to his wagon. Cooper claimed that as he and O'Malley walked to the police station, they were met by his associate A.C. McNeil. The only way the younger lawyer could have joined them so quickly was if he had been watching from concealment, as the Cap'n would charge. Kirk was visited in his guard cabin by Johnny Allmendinger of the family that owned part of the shore and by a relative of his, John Shrickel. Police said these men saw McManners, Hoeldtke and a third Streeter guard heading their way. Kirk hurried out with a fellow guard for the shore owners.

There were now two lines of men with guns facing each other possibly four hundred feet apart. Streeter guard William Force maintained that he was not among them and stated in an affidavit that from Lake Shore Drive he could see about eight men from Cooper's camp and they had fired first. The men on each side were bundled in thick coats, making it uncertain who was firing. According to Force, who may not have been trustworthy, Streeter told his men a week earlier to shoot any of Cooper's people attempting to cause trouble.[60]

The two lines of gunmen discharged up to two dozen shots but stopped when Kirk was wounded in the head and fell near death in the falling snow. The Cap'n was arrested in his wagon-tent. Though in the worst trouble of his life, he still had a cigar in his mouth and a plug hat resting far back on his hairless head. He denied taking part in the shooting and even knocking Cooper down earlier. His mood turned somber when told that Kirk had died at around midnight in Passavant Hospital without regaining consciousness.

On February 28, Streeter, McManners, Hoeldtke and Force were indicted for murder.

11

The no-man's land was filling up. In 1901, needing a headquarters for its operations, the Chicago Dock and Canal Company erected a six-story masonry and timber building at 337–51 East Illinois Street in the modern numbering and the next year constructed a companion building. These were possibly the first commercial structures in Streeterville.

But the city's era of farseeing planning ended on March 4, 1902, when Potter Palmer died in his castle overlooking mansions and the barren land. His legacy was a continuous fortune for Bertha and his fellow investors in the Lake Shore Drive development. Money from rents went to such institutions as the Art Institute of Chicago, what is now the Chicago History Museum, United Charities of Chicago, the Chicago Commons Association to aid the poor, Children's Memorial Hospital, the Legal Aid Society of Chicago and the Home for the Friendless. In addition, some rents John V. Farwell collected from his seven North Side apartment buildings no doubt were donated to his favorite institutions, the Moody Bible Institute and the YMCA of Chicago.[61]

Soon after Palmer's death, the second stage of his Lake Shore Drive plan was realized, as a few mansions only ten years old were replaced by tall cooperatives with controlled tenancy. Designed by sought-after architects, these residential spires offered floor plans in French, and rents were so prohibitive they guaranteed that only the right sort of people would move in. Everyone knew what "the right sort" meant.

It might have been that Streeter had been tolerated because the unsightliness of his camp and his ridiculous, circus master clothes—or costumes—discouraged rival developers. What did it matter, since the murder indictment and other charges meant that the pest would be gotten rid of shortly.

On June 14, Judge Marcus Kavanaugh quashed the Cap'n's indictment for selling lots, since he was in enough trouble. Then he was found guilty of assaulting Cooper, but the fine was waived. On June 26, 1902, the Cap'n's murder trial began in the criminal court building at Illinois and Hubbard Streets.[62] Testimony was not about who shot Kirk, something no one could say, but on whether Streeter legally possessed the land he and his men were protecting. A shouting match erupted when General Fitz-Simons called out from his seat that Streeter had threatened to shoot Cooper, which was probably true but hearsay.

Tempers stayed heated as questioning turned to the Cap'n's arrival in the city. "Didn't you stop me from getting my boat off the shore the time I was shipwrecked?" Streeter yelled to Fitz-Simons. "And didn't you burn down one of my shanties, you and a lot of policemen?" As the exchange continued, the contractor rose up from the spectator section and had to be plunked back down by three bailiffs. The next day, Streeter spewed a number of lies in evident panic at the likelihood of conviction, such as claiming Hoeldtke and Force had been secretly working for the shore owners.[63] Then as the Cap'n sat out deliberations, a lawyer in the nearly empty courtroom tugged at his sleeve and asked, "Will you take $2,000 for your interest in 'the district'?"

The Cap'n sat up and replied, "Two million dollars—not a cent less. We're sellin' lots same as ever and no $2,000 will ever buy me out."

After thirty-four hours of deliberations, jurors on the night of July 16 declared themselves deadlocked in the cases of Streeter, McManners and Hoeldtke. They acquitted William Force because he had given state's evidence.[64]

Streeter returned to his land with murder charges still over him. That warm summer, the North Side was too noisy for residents in the fancy new apartments, with much of the racket coming from beer gardens, saloons and Clark Street music halls. Forever with the moneyed class in mind, Mayor Carter Harrison II solved the problem with selective license revocations, closing every raucous place and beginning the Near North Side's tradition of reserve.[65]

On the afternoon of August 12, less than a month after the first murder trial, Streeter was called to the city hall office of Police Chief Francis O'Neil on a ruse. Next, a police inspector, a lieutenant, a squad of patrolmen and five deputized workmen moved onto the disputed acres. The Cap'n realized that O'Neil did not want to see him—ever—and a policeman escorted him back to the district. Louisa Healy's attorney, Wells, facetiously told the bruisers dismantling the McMannerses' shack, "You are the only gentlemen who have been in the 'deestrict' for a long time." The ruffians also ripped out Maria's beet and lettuce garden as she and Streeter uttered so many curses that the *Chicago Tribune* wryly noted that repeating their comments "would exhaust all the lower case 'ds' in a printing shop."[66]

The Streeters relocated to another section of the reclaimed land but must have known it would only be temporary. On September 20, Captain Revere once more served notice that everyone living in the district must vacate within six hours. Speaking from his wagon, the Cap'n declared: "Doherty ——, this is my home, and I am here to stay." The Cap'n was arrested and disarmed when he and two supporters started moving furniture back.

In the mid-autumn of 1902, Maria was bumped by a streetcar somewhere on the North Side and refused to go to a hospital. As her injuries worsened, her husband had to raise money in vaudeville without her, even though she was on the bill. Despite his concern, he appeared daily for a week at the Metropolitan Theater to joke with the audience and talk about his fights with the millionaires.[67]

Since transcripts of his second murder trial were destroyed for shelf room, we have only a spotty newspaper account of the proceedings, such as when Streeter exasperated Judge Arthur Chetlain by trying to act as his own lawyer on November 24, 1902. The Cap'n defied a young prosecutor with the memorable name of Frederick Fake by refusing to answer any question that made him uncomfortable. His evasions and lies harmed his case more than Fake could have. Jurors deliberated in a hotel until nearly sunup, then convicted the three defendants of the lesser charge of manslaughter. The jury recommended leniency for Hoeldtke, but Streeter and McManners were given "indefinite" terms, potentially meaning life in prison. The Cap'n told a newsman, "It only goes to show that when a lot of millionaires get together and get the help of the state, the liberty of man ain't safe."[68]

12

Maria, at sixty, was walking just off Streeterville on February 11, 1903—perhaps to visit her husband in jail—when she could no longer stand the pain. Her attractive niece Nora "Nonny" Hollst helped her to a barn behind 588 East Chicago Avenue to rest about three hundred feet from where she and the Cap'n had been shipwrecked. Ma, never a complainer, said she knew that she was dying. That night, the Cap'n was taken to a jail office and told of her death. With a shrug, he said to a reporter, "I suppose they're satisfied." He meant the millionaires. "We were a credit to the Deestrict, Mariar and me." Two deputy sheriffs accompanied the Cap'n to her funeral Mass in Holy Name Cathedral, a few blocks from the district. He was returned to the jail after Maria's burial at Mount Olivet Cemetery. Next, N.K. Fairbank died in his home at 18th and Michigan on March 28.

Under state law, Streeter should have been taken to Joliet State Prison soon after sentencing, but officials had let him remain in county jail while he appealed his conviction. An Illinois Supreme Court panel held on January 13, 1904, that legal issues cited by his lawyers did not call for a new interpretation of the law. Ten days later, the Cap'n arrived at the gates of the pre–Civil War penitentiary a broken man in shabby clothes. Later, he accepted an invitation to speak to the assembled female inmates. Allowed to wear his own clothing for the appearance, he sang a song from his childhood.

In mid-autumn of that year, African American lawyer William Anderson came across a technicality with the potential of unlocking the old man's cell, and Streeter offered him $30,000 if he succeeded even though he had no idea how to come up with the money. Anderson explained that an 1895 state law required an automatic parole hearing within one year of conviction for felonies other than murder, and Streeter had been found guilty of manslaughter. The Cap'n was in jail for more than a year, and he had never appeared before a parole board. Many jurists would be justified in ruling that the law did not apply since Streeter had remained there at his own request, so Anderson's filing a writ of habeas corpus would be a roll of the dice, but his client had nothing to lose.

A hearing on November 14, 1904, was over in a few minutes. Judge Edward Dunne ruled that he had no choice but to free Streeter. Shouts erupted, and editors sent reporters rushing to the courthouse because not one newspaper had covered what had seemed like a routine hearing. For once, the Cap'n declined to speak to newsmen before he was conveyed to an apartment leased by Nonny and her husband at 29th Street and Cottage Grove Avenue.[69] Later, he returned to Indiana, where he felt more comfortable.

Streeter, who was anywhere from sixty-three to seventy years old, having suitably mourned Maria's loss, surprised everyone by marrying nineteen-year-old Mary or Mamie Collins from his hometown of Montrose, Michigan. The ceremony was performed in South Bend on April 21, 1904. Mary probably was the teenage girl seen at several of his court appearances and possibly escorted his ninety-year-old mother to the jail for her one visit. Whatever Mary may have looked like, the Cap'n must have wooed her with his Cleveland document. He seemed more amused than heartbroken by her departure three months later. In June 1905, Mary filed for divorce in Cook County and brought with her a bogus log of supposed daily beatings as a record of Streeter's cruelty. Her petition was dismissed, no doubt as an obvious gold-digging scam, so she and Streeter remained married, although they never met again, something that would become important later.[70]

Somewhere around South Bend, Streeter met and claimed to have married Elmira Lockwood, a divorcee with two adult sons. She was the daughter of a moderately well-off farm couple, so of course Streeter told everyone her father had been a prominent judge. She preferred the name "Elma," and her bridegroom affectionately called her "Ma." The Cap'n's final life partner was the most likable but dullest of his four wives, legal and otherwise. She believed his tall tales and enjoyed cooking and the company of young people.

After an unrecorded period, Streeter reemerged in July 1907 while fixing up an old steamboat in South Bend with lumber he bought on credit. The next two years saw several Chicago-style clashes with local Indiana authorities, and the Cap'n was once locked up for assaulting an officer. When he returned to Chicago with Ma, he saw that the disputed land had not been improved in his absence, looking as if it had been plowed up. Despite the many mansions and several new apartment towers, the *Record-Herald* said that "Streeterville" had not lost its "evil name" as a dump heap, with stagnant water filling clay pits that had been dug for building material.[71]

Rattling and coughing motor cars now shared the drive with horse-drawn carriages, and the looming residential skyscrapers fit in with quickening times. When the nine-story Marshall Apartments, named for fashionable architect Benjamin Marshall, opened in October 1906, it was described as "typical" of the new perpendicular homes going up in the Gold Coast. Marshall rents were set at an unprecedented $4,200 a year. Its French classicism was guaranteed to impress friends, and being at 23 Lake Shore Drive (later 1100 North Lake Shore Drive), it was just two blocks from the evermore anachronistic Palmer castle.

Walls in the Marshall were paneled in English oak, and the *H*-shaped floor plan showed a reception hall, an octagonal dining room, a large salon and an "orangerie," a greenhouse to protect decorative plants. An apartment there also featured a library, a billiard room and three maid's rooms. A butler's quarters was optional. Small doors opened onto fruit and wine closets. You reached the top floor not by an elevator but *l'ascenseur*. Strange that the word should suggest an ascension into the clouds, because Chicago newsman Ben Hecht wrote that for a reporter nothing was out of bounds but heaven and Lake Shore Drive. The Marshall's first tenant was Samuel Insull, the British-born financier who had been encouraged to leave Philadelphia on suspicion of selling worthless stock. Behaving himself in Chicago, Insull became enormously wealthy by purchasing railroads and utilities and gave the city its opera house.

Attractive Benjamin Marshall was clean-shaven, as most up-and-comers were in the new century, and took long strides because he was a designer in a hurry. Lacking training in architecture, he was an adapter rather than an innovator, picking elements from Renaissance, Gothic, Tudor, Second Empire French styles—whatever might be comfortable in the setting. Other architects planned nearby buildings that were compatible with his. He was often seen in a standout white suit, sometimes with a beautiful woman at his arm. Marshall not only moved among the rich like a Jay Gatsby, but he also knew how to excite the interest of the carriage set.

Marshall designed some of the most admired residential buildings and hotels in the Gold Coast. By stressing élan, his influence would help bridge

Streeterville's stagnant period, when much of the district was taken up by uninspiring four-square brick buildings in the 1930s through the '50s, to the luxury buildings of the 1960s through the '80s. All were built within Palmer's concept, but some on the fringe were intended for the upper middle class rather than the elite, such as the Raymond Flats at Walton Place and the former Pine Street.

Streeter's latest neighbors in 1907 were Medill McCormick, publisher of the *Chicago Tribune*, at 23 Lake Shore Drive; Ogden Trevor McClurg, a descendant of a Civil War brevet general; and wealthy Chicago publisher Alexander McClurg, whose company printed the first *Tarzan* book. The sophistication of Elm Street Apartments, at 1130 Lake Shore Drive—opened in 1910—seemed to snub the mansions close by, and so it was elsewhere on East Elm and other streets ending at the drive. Ogden Trevor McClurg traded his rather new mansion for a large luxury apartment at 999 Lake Shore Drive, where tenants usually held "receiving Tuesdays." Jumping ahead, Prohibition gangster Terry Druggan longed to live on the drive as proof that he had crashed society, and so in 1925 he leased an apartment at 999 in his wife's name. His bootleg business ended with a tax trial a few years later.

Across from future Oak Street beach was a Marshall-designed apartment building at 1100 LSD. To enter, one needed to be cleared by a doorman on the watch for salesmen and thieves. The plush flats trimmed with mahogany and oak had a billiard room and a passageway listed as "help's hall," and every floor had a laundry. This was the epitome of convenience at the time and the inspiration for the managed development of all East Lake Shore Drive.

Building designer Robert Seeley DeGolyer, ranking in the respectable second tier of Chicago architects, drew plans for the cooperative next door, at 1120 Lake Shore Drive. A brochures tells us that it "is in the short half mile of lake frontage reputed to be the finest residential section in the world." DeGoyler also planned the co-op at 200 East Pearson Street, described by promoters as an elegant "palazzo" gracing the progressively more proper Streeterville, its "evil name" replaced by chic respectability in just a few years.

Even though high-rise living was in vogue, interiors still reflected the tastes of half a century earlier. When young architect Frank Lloyd Wright visited his first opulent tower, the Elm Street Apartments, he beheld marble floors, Gothic tapestries, elaborate ironwork, a library with a sixteen-foot ceiling and, in this age of electricity, candles illuminating every room. "I utterly failed to imagine entering it other than in costume," he remarked. Excesses in the mansions and newly opened cooperatives shaped Wright's conception of simple, round or angular, even slab-like, homes as part of the Prairie School of architecture.

Other large chic apartment buildings sprang up at 936, 950, 199, 1150, 1200 (the Stewart Apartments), 1220 and 1240 Lake Shore Drive, all in the original numbering. Rents at the Stewart, at Division Street and the Drive, just outside Streeterville, initially went up to $6,000 a year. Some families leased an apartment there or in a neighboring tower for only a few months a year between trips to the East Coast or Europe. Among later residents of the Stewart would be a grandson of the department store king Marshall Field. Marshall Field III was a banker who founded the *Chicago Sun*, forerunner of the *Sun-Times*. Over at 1550 lived Victor Lawson, the crusading force behind the *Chicago Daily News* in its muckraking heyday.

The development of Lake Shore Drive can be told in dollar signs as well as in names. In 1882, the value of the mushy land had been $150 a front foot. By 1892, when the fabled thoroughfare was still incomplete and when there were questions about the ownership of sections, the same land was valued at $800. By 1909, only the city's wealthiest could live there.

Residents in aging upscale districts now wanted an address on the drive or one of its side streets such as Elm or Pearson. They could transfer easily from South Michigan Avenue, South Ashland Boulevard and West Washington Street because Chicago had never evolved a social order that would have held interlocking families together. Reflecting the subsequent decline, the John Gates mansion at 29th and Michigan had cost $300,000 a few decades earlier but in 1908 it sold for just $65,000. Values in the area would decline further by the year, and the economic misfortune of the South Side was that no one seemed interested in clearing a large area for managed commercial ventures, as on the Near North Side.[72]

While some authorities were still questioning the legality of building the drive with taxpayer money on private landfill, agents fronting for the still-undisclosed shore owners of the 1880s had extolled how a landscaped thoroughfare at the lakefront would create a refuge for the common people. But in succeeding years, the owners and the park commission did nothing to encourage public use of the boulevard or what could have been wading areas. The Lincoln Park Commission had to be threatened with legal action before it erected pedestrian bridges over Lake Shore Drive motor traffic, as if the agency were trying to keep the drive as exclusive as possible. Authorities did not even mind when construction crews were careless in scooping up sand along the submerged part of the sloping shore. A teenager drowned before hundreds of people in 1915 when he stepped into a deep hole that had been gouged two years earlier but never filled.

One of the forces bringing handfuls of families to the pale-yellow sands on hot days was former chief city attorney Charles Walker, an outdoor enthusiast. The *Chicago Legal News* looked back in 1920 at how "at a time when no one except small boys used the lake for bathing [wading and swimming], he called attention to the benefits to be derived from utilizing as a public play ground the sandy shores of the lake and now Chicago's bathing beaches rank among the finest in the world." In 1922–23 the city raised the lake floor at Oak Street with sand from elsewhere because the bulge created by Fitz-Simons's greed had made the water too deep for family enjoyment.[73]

The tangled story of how small private beaches north and south of the reclaimed land were turned into a nearly unbroken chain of sandy public recreation areas belongs elsewhere. All people cared about was that from May to mid-September, the more adventuresome could swim to the breakwater and back from the end of both Fullerton Avenue and Oak Street, although there would be no lifeguards until 1916. The city allowed a few wheeled concession stands at the two beaches, but many people brought picnic baskets and sat on blankets between their dips into the lake. The millionaires never seem to have complained about the commonplace sunbathers. But then, their yachts could sail far beyond the breakwater.

The McClurg family caused a stir among fellow Gold Coasters by breaching Palmer's unwritten master plan and building a printing plant just off the lake. Shore owners made no public protest, but the Cap'n, called by his lawyer "the King of Streeterville," filed a $5 million ejection suit against the wealthy family. Magistrates and judges routinely treated the Cap'n's court filings as a joke, but this time Circuit Court Judge John Gibbons responded by sending letters to the city attorney and Illinois attorney general. Referring to a U.S. Supreme Court ruling on riparian rights in a Mississippi case, Gibbons told them: "While some property owners on the North Shore may have acquired vested rights, the great bulk of the lake front property, both along the North and South shore, may be saved by prompt action.… Whether what is left of the lake shore may be saved or lost to the people depends entirely upon the action or failure to act of the attorney general and the city of Chicago corporation counsel." Judge Gibbons estimated the value of the land at $27 million.

Whether from peer pressure or a court decision lost to us, the new printing plant came down. But its temporary presence had shown that Palmer's grand plan could no longer be sustained. Not while a new generation of shore owners subdivided and leased their vacant property to commercial interests. Several near-shore factories, especially between East Ontario and East Ohio Streets, were operating six days a week. One of them, the Curtiss Candy Company, produced popular Kandy Kake bars, later named Baby Ruth, at 337 East Illinois Street.

In addition, Streeterville received windblown smoke from the nearby Kirk Soap Company on North Water Street, now part of Wacker Drive. Other blemishes on the landscape were the Pugh Terminal Warehouse, at 435 East Illinois, owned by trustees of the Ogden Slip; the Mill Construction Company; and the Pittsburgh Coal Company dock at the mouth of the river. These factories and docks were interspersed with a few "boat houses"—that is, squatter and fishermen's shacks—and by mid-1909, a number of "for sale" signs went up as the millionaires' row entered a decline. Palmer's vision had stopped only halfway.

The city standardized all addresses in 1909 except for Lake Shore Drive. In deference to the rich inhabitants, these were changed only years later. In August 1909, the Cap'n was seen patching up a steamboat resting in "a tadpole ditch" a few miles south of Joliet and living in a lumber shed. He was asked about the recent death of eighty-three-year-old John V. Farwell but had nothing of interest to say about the last of his personal enemies. From now on, his foes would be just the Chicago Title and Trust Company and whoever filed individual legal action against him. In early September, Streeter was back to thumbing his nose at the millionaires from his place somewhere on the former sand land. We know of his return only because he was caught killing three ducks belonging to someone named Barney Kinlespire. The Cap'n claimed that each of them had accidentally caught itself in his rabbit trap. The newspapers did not carry the outcome of the case.

Streeter and Ma entered the Motor Age in July 1910. As he explained it in an aside in a misconduct trial: "One night while we were at a theater a joker stile [stole] the truck [large car] and took it to Streeterville. I found it and had it moved" off East Ontario Street. After fining him $150 for disturbing the peace, the judge lectured him on his "wild and riotous conduct." Streeter responded: "I ain't agreein' with you jedge, [but] Streeterville won't never have a chamber of commerce until it has a cabaret. This is a frontier town and it's got to go though its red-blooded youth. You gotta start with entertainment."[74]

Around this time, young Everett Guy Ballard met Streeter as many people did, at gunpoint. Ballard heard, "Get out of here!" and told the

Lake Shore Drive in 1910. The developers were keeping the marsh as a wasteland as long as Cap'n Streeter claimed the land. *Chicago History Museum.*

Cap'n he was a lawyer but was not representing anyone. The Cap'n put his old rifle down and explained that he had been pestered by surveyors wanting to plot yet another fence to hem him in. Ballard apparently left without explaining his visit: to gather material for a book about the legendary squatter. At least forty Streeter investors reacted to the new fence by forming the Property Owners Association and, in 1910, empowering attorney Samuel Herron to oust respectable residents such as the McClurgs from their mansions. A judge dismissed their action but noted in letters to the Illinois attorney general and the city council, the modern name of the common council, that in his background inquiry he was informed the land was now worth up to $90 million.

That same year, Farwell heirs were among investors in a six-story luxury residential building at 33 East Bellevue Place, called the Chandler Apartments after developer Buckingham Chandler. The wrought-iron entrance canopy was roofed with polished copper, and the marble main staircase, graced with mahogany railings, led to a fountain in an inner courtyard. Dining rooms were paneled variously in mahogany, birch, oak or walnut, and the fireplace mantels were hand-carved.

In contrast to the wealthy moving into the area, Streeter was still unable to pay attorney Anderson the promised $30,000 for getting him out of prison. The sheriff's office prepared to put the Cap'n's claim up for auction by dividing the Streeterville camp into 270 lots covering thirty-five square blocks. They began at Hubbard Street near the river and went north to Oak Street and from the future North Michigan Avenue east to the lake. On December 20, 1910, a deputy mounted a box inside a county building entrance and announced to nearly five hundred hopefuls, "Now, let it be understood that the county does not guarantee a title to the land. But those who want it, can have it." In an aside to a reporter, the deputy said, "The titles to this property are figuratively a thousand to one."

A junk dealer jumped off his wagon and shoved his way closer while saying, "I want a block. I want a block." For $105 cash, he obtained the Cap'n's claim to seventy lots fronting Chicago Avenue. Less desirable sections went for $12. Anderson had expected the lots to go for $5 to $10 apiece, but the auction netted $1,674. Then Streeter went back to his home in a somehow-acquired old wooden streetcar that had a dozen windows on each side. He had turned it into his winter quarters and for some reason no longer had his "housemobile."[75]

Most of the business leaders who had revitalized Chicago after the Great Fire were now dead—including Palmer, Fairbank, Farwell and Marshall Field—and their less energetic successors did not share their spirit of cooperating in enterprises benefiting the public at least indirectly. Civil engineer Lyman E. Cooley of the sanitary district had something like this in mind when he lamented in 1911 that although "Chicago was a child of destiny, of opportunity," because of the lake, it was losing lake-borne commerce by "our sins of omission," such as not constructing a harbor that could accommodate steel-hulled freighters. "We were so busy jostling each other in an effort to get our gunny sacks under the [grain] spout…that we imagined all of our prosperity was due to some innate quality of citizenship rather than a pre-ordained condition"—the lake and the city's waterways. The neglect hampered the city's economic growth while enriching speculators in lakefront real estate.[76]

And something else was being lost by the evolution of Lake Shore Drive from mansions to apartment towers. No one held charity balls anymore, and no one was leading by example. Instead of society, there were now hundreds of rich people living separately, their tastes and good works known to just a few, and exclusive clubs were just places for playing cards rather than trading ideas. At the time, society architect Benjamin Marshall adopted a sideline of selectively speculating in real estate. Probably sensing that Oak Street Beach would become a lure once it was improved, in 1911 he began developing the short but significant East Lake Shore Drive from what was then the southern end of the road, toward downtown. Even today, these few blocks from the lake to North Michigan Avenue have the most rarefied air in the city, as detailed later.[77]

Montgomery Ward died of pneumonia in December 1913 at the age of seventy. He had fought harder for the public than any other person in Chicago—the entire unspoiled lakefront is his legacy—but he left this world unappreciated and misunderstood. At the time of his funeral, the modern city was largely what it is now and at the peak of its cultural significance.

Earlier that year, Guy Ballard visited Streeter several times to take down—and embellish—the squatter's already embellished and invented recollections. The Cap'n had agreed to a book because he needed money, probably unaware how little most authors make. The lawyer-writer arranged his visits to coincide with mealtimes because Ma was an excellent cook. Ballard and Streeter entered into an oral agreement to produce a book, "an instructive and entertaining work" that would correct "many garbled and inaccurate accounts of his life," according to a once-lost deposition.

Streeter promised Ballard a thirty-three-dollar retainer in several installments as the storytelling and writing continued. The squatter may have had intended *Captain Streeter, Pioneer* to concentrate on his childhood in frontier Michigan, since he had reasons for not giving the whole truth about his claim to the Chicago shore, but his collaborator testified that he wanted to fashion "a novel" about the subject's battling the millionaires. Ballard stated in the deposition that he always read to Streeter what he had written, but possibly not all that he had written.

Printers William Goulding and Cecil Emory agreed to run off five thousand copies for $1,000. In early June 1914, Streeter got hold of the typescript and was outraged. He went to his collaborator and demanded that every scrap of paper be taken from the printers and turned over to him. When Ballard refused, the Cap'n went to court, and a deposition was taken. But rather than risking a trial, the two sides compromised. With input from Streeter, Ballard rewrote passages, possibly ones describing his hero's confrontations with the rich and influential. The friction and the fiction made *Captain Streeter, Pioneer* a mixture of reminiscences of a Michigan childhood and a jumbled fanciful story laid out on Chicago's shore. Its lies are the primary basis for all the inaccurate accounts about Streeter written over the next eighty years, since the millionaires never gave their own version. The give-and-take between partners was so satisfactory that Streeter used Ballard as his civil attorney for years.

13

In 1915, the enclave known as the District of Lake Michigan—that is, what remained after the area was landscaped and various mansions and apartment stacks had gone up—supported the largest and most diverse population in its squatter history. Besides the Cap'n and Ma, there was an unknown number of unauthorized residents, including the late Maria's niece Nora "Nonny" Hollst and her tall husband, Herman. They had left their home in North Dakota to help the Streeters as long as the couple might need them.

Nonny was said to have "adopted" thirteen boys and girls in the city, probably meaning that she accepted them in temporary foster care. One of her charges was seventeen-year-old Henry DeCarmaker, whose last name might have been Streeter's corruption of Carmichael. The boy lived with the Hollsts in the old trolley, which possibly had been abandoned in the changeover from horse-drawn streetcars to motorized ones. For sport, the boy shot jackrabbits in the weeds with an air gun. The still-attractive Nonny volunteered as a county probation officer and did missionary work among the poor. Another citizen of the sands was aging widow Levonia Edwards, who liked to be called "Mrs. Eddy." She had left her North Side home to live in a Streeterville shack for one dollar a month. The most usual person on the sand land was probably Chris Mantis, a Greek man who operated a fruit and candy store next to the single-story brick building Alderman Cullerton had built for the Streeters.

Shacks, tents and a streetcar cluttering the land were one thing, but what pulled the trigger for the Healy estate was some sort of "windmill" the Cap'n and his supporters erected. We have to guess what it was. Perhaps it was some sort of informal tower construction, in that Streeter had promised reporters that one day the district would feature something to rival Eiffel's. In 1915, lawyers for heirs of the portraitist demanded action, and Streeter's people moved whatever it was a short distance—three inches, someone joked. Unamused, four sheriff's deputies seized the Cap'n at what a newspaper called "the Broadway of Streeterville," the foot of Chicago Avenue, and a judge sentenced him to spend sixty days in jail.

Unlike Maria, Ma was never comfortable living outdoors, so she managed a rooming house somewhere on the North Side. She seems to have lived for baking pies in the back of the couple's little food store and bringing them to her tenants. The district had no running water or electricity, and illumination was only by moon and a few kerosene lamps. Life must have been reasonably pleasant in good weather. For music, residents could sing or crank up a gasoline-run mechanical organ. There were no taxes to pay, no alarm clocks and unlimited vistas of lake and sky. For a brief moment, this was Chicago's Forest of Arden.[78]

After an unusually rainy summer in 1915, residents enjoyed a dry and color-filled autumn unaware of forces gathering against them. The trouble began on September 14, when Detective Sergeant William Freeman conducted a weapons raid and his officers pistol-whipped the old squatter as he resisted. Worse trouble lay ahead. Mayor William Hale Thompson posed as a moralist even though he had been put in office by the prostitution and gambling interests, and now he pretended outrage at Sunday liquor sales. He started a crackdown just after beer became available in Streeterville.

Mrs. Eddy claimed that after evangelist Billy Sunday's huge revival meeting in the city she told the Cap'n, "You must fight the Devil with his own arms. You must sell beer by the truck load." Ma evidently agreed that selling bottled beer with sandwiches seven days a week was a fine idea. After all, no one bothered Chicago's numerous small "tipping houses," where drinking was done, but they were not saloons. There is no mention in any of the sources of the Cap'n ever drinking himself.

Relishing publicity, Streeter threw a large outdoor party attended by future mayor Anton Cermak the first Sunday after stocking the brew. The Cap'n lacked a liquor license for dealing in the beer any day of the week and should have known there would be trouble. On Tuesday, October 12, four officers in civilian clothes headed by Detective Sergeant George Cudmore came by. This "big brute of a man," said Streeter, entered the store off Chestnut with two officers posing as his friends while two others remained outside. The strangers asked for sandwiches and beer from the approximately 150 bottles on the shelves. After being served, Cudmore said, "We've got you now, Captain!" While Streeter stalled them, Henry DeCarmaker came in with tobacco and slipped him a revolver, which the Cap'n concealed behind his waistband. When he reached for it, Cudmore shouted, "Stop!"

"Stop, nothing!"

All three policemen wrestled with him for the pistol. Ma rushed in, grabbed Streeter's gun from him to "save his life," and somehow it went off, taking a strip of flesh from Cudmore's shoulder. Another officer joined in, and all four fought the septuagenarian beer-seller to the floor. When the Cap'n was brought outside, matronly Ma slammed the door and said she would kill anyone trying to enter. She slipped out a back window undetected by a guard posted in front. The Cap'n was treated at the police station near Chicago and State by a police surgeon, and when he was released in the morning, he linked arms with Ma and joked, "Hooray, the flag still waves!"[79]

A few weeks after the fight, an acquaintance passed along word that a certain James Pugh was interested in buying rights to a portion of Streeterville's claim for $2,000. But the Cap'n was immediately suspicious. Streeter's suspicions increased when Pugh raised the offer to $8,000. No one learned whether he really was a real estate speculator or had been acting on behalf of a shore owner wanting to ensnare him.

A headline in the *Sunday Chicago Tribune* on November 14 read "MONTE CARLO IN STREETERVILLE!" The jocular article was about a Thomas Hennessy, possibly Streeter's bondsman, paying the Cap'n a sum to build a friendly gambling and Sunday drinking operation in the back of the little store. The Cap'n said of the potential conflict with Mayor Thompson, "When these reactionaries quit cloggin' the wheels of progress we'll have a nation out of Streeterville yet." He must have doubted anyone would take him seriously, but the new mayor refused to be humiliated.

That very evening, Nonny and Herman Hollst were trying to stay warm in their trolley apartment. After Ma put fourteen pies out to cool, she and the Cap'n served a few customers who dropped by their grocery to chat. As police officers gathered, mansion residents must have looked out their curtained windows to watch what was about to happen. At 9:00 p.m., a heavyset man in street clothes stood by the grocery/home and removed his hat. At that signal, two motorized prisoner wagons rolled in to flank the little brick building, possibly with an officer clinging to the back handgrips, and

Cap'n Streeter, "Ma" and Spot sit out the 1915 raid. The couple do not look surprised that the end had come. *Chicago History Museum.*

then the rear doors flew open. The wagons usually held four to eight officers, but now they were crammed with a total of more than thirty.

Mantis, the man who sold soft drinks next to the Streeter grocery/home, tried to stop twenty patrolmen from rushing into the Cap'n's place. An officer struck him in the jaw, and then, said a newspaper, "beer bottles crashed to the floor" and gunfire erupted. Mrs. Eddy alleged that the officers just threw a side door open "and started shooting." One slug went over Ma's head and another grazed Streeter's scalp. For no known reason, bluecoats outside fired into the old trolley where the Hollsts lay in a makeshift bed. Herman would say later that some policemen barged in and "I heard a rattle of shots." A slug hit his wife in the hip. Herman protested, only to be struck in the face.

As the Cap'n was pulled out of the store, Ma said, "Blood was streaming down his face and his eyes were closed, and they was pounding him over the head with their revolvers." The battered squatter joined the rest of the prisoners in the paddy wagon. All eight were bystanders, and at least one lived in the Gold Coast. While they were being processed, officers returned to the little grocery/home and took everything from cigars to a chest of documents, then went to the kitchen and smashed whatever could. They carried away Ma's pies, and one lawman poured gasoline on both beds. He must have intended to light a fire, but another officer told him there was not enough time.[80] City custodian DeWitt Cregier Jr., whose mother owned land near where the attack occurred, said that Sherman Spitzer, the title company vice president as well as an assistant city attorney, told him there had been an order to pull down the Cap'n's home. "They intended to dynamite it, I think," Cregier said to a reporter. When asked for confirmation, Spitzer was evasive.

The *Tribune* reported that the raiders confiscated 8,100 full bottles, probably containing beer from Streeter's place and soda pop from Mantis's; five rifles; Henry's air gun; a revolver; and several hundred rounds of ammunition. The beer was turned over to the city custodian's office, and the illegally seized documents were illegally given to the title company rather than being handed back to Streeter or impounded as evidence. The Cap'n received no medical attention until Ballard arrived at the station with a private physician.

After saloonkeeper "Spike" Kennedy posted bail that night, the Cap'n returned to his pillaged home with a reporter. He struck a match to view the destruction. The floor was strewn with broken bottles from his stock, crockery lay shattered, gasoline soaked the beds and missing were his document trunk, fifteen loaves of bread, two crates of eggs,and supposedly eight hundred cigars. "Now I see what the raid was all about," he lamented. "They wanted the things that prove the right I have to my property—the Indian grants, the government patent rights, my soldier scrip and all."

The Cap'n suggested the raid had been planned after he refused Pugh's offer. Speaking as his lawyer, Ballard said with a strong element of truth that "in the last 30 years there has been not one mayor or a judge or a police chief who would have taken such an action as taken today." Crews tore down what remained of the Mantis store and carried off the clumps of brick and mortar in motor wagons with reinforced wooden sides five feet high. The men started knocking down Streeter's home as well but for some reason were told to stop.

14

S treeter's trial on a charge of assault with intent to kill Detective Sergeant Freeman during the September weapons raid began on November 16, 1915. His lawyers contended that police had no authority for the raid, and the Cap'n drew laughter when he objected to the way the prosecutor was questioning him. "Attorney," he said, "introduce into evidence those documents showing the meandering line of the lake." A prosecutor named Herron ignored him.

When Streeter wasn't in court during his trial, he was performing at the McVickers Theater downtown. He was paid $1,000 for the week of November 22, giving his version of the generation-long battle as a film clip of the Gold Coast played on a screen behind him. He then introduced Ma, they bowed and the orchestra struck up the national anthem. He apparently did this five times a day.

The assault jurors were asked on November 23 to walk from the criminal court building to the formerly disputed land a few blocks away. After the twelve men returned to their chairs, Streeter delivered his own closing statement. "Gentlemen of the jury," came his high voice, "you have heard how these big duffers of policemen fell on me, beat me, kicked me when I was down. Now this sort of thing has been going on for thirty years."

"Object!" Herron called out.

"Well, it's true, ain't it? But let it go at that. I'll stick to the evidence that shows for the last thirty years the police have been jumping on me but I never took the law into my own hands....They have burned down

12 houses in the deestrict," including the Fairbank action with the police as observers, "and tried to kill me and railroad me into the penitentiary to get me out of the way. But I'm not seeking your sympathy. All I want is justice." After deliberating less than two and a half hours, they found him not guilty. As the Cap'n embraced Ma in the corridor, he said, "Gol dang it, I'm some lawyer, ain't I?"[81]

An uneasy quiet followed the trial. No one interfered with squatters conducting their daily routines. In 1916, the city improved Oak Street Beach at Fitz-Simons's land bulge and made it one of the few splendors of Chicago. The cut-rate Barry excursion ship company bused customers from the former Pine Street pier to the newly opened Municipal Pier (Navy Pier) off Indiana Street (Grand Avenue) to compete with the larger Goodrich line. In 1918, Bertha Palmer passed away. An unknown portion of her estimated $18 million estate came from Streeterville rents.

That same year, John Allmendinger of the family that first suggested something like Lake Shore Drive accomplished what the millionaires declined to do. He forced the Cap'n into a showdown. Allmendinger's first step was to assert that he was related by marriage to the Kinzie family of early Chicago settlers and therefore was entitled to additional acres. In response to his lawsuit to remove the Cap'n, Judge Merritt Pinckney formally declared the Cleveland document "a clumsy forgery," as federal authorities had maintained for years. With that out of the way, Allmendinger's suit to evict Streeter proceeded to trial. Attorneys from the large law firm of DeFrees, Buckingham and Eton declared that virtually everything the Cap'n ever did in Chicago was illegal. Representing himself, Streeter was funny and colorful when others would have been wary and restrained.

Acting on behalf of Allmendinger and other legal owners was title company vice president and city attorney Sherman Spitzer. "Ever live in Washington?" he asked in hopes of having the Cap'n's speak about his postwar desertion from a tent hospital in Washington, D.C.

"Yes."

"How long?"

"Well, I didn't die there." One can almost hear the courtroom chuckles. "Say," the Cap'n added, "why don't you ask me where I resided?" Instead, the questioning meandered, as if Spitzer were trying to make the small bald man look either foolish or a liar. When asked about the late Maria, Streeter often referred to her as his wife, but not this time. He testified that she had been his "companion." Even so, the judgment went against him, and he was given a few weeks to appeal but did nothing. Fight had finally gone out of him.

The Streeters in their partly demolished brick home were quite a sight for swimmers and bathers using Oak Street Beach. A 1920s crowd estimate said the beach sometimes saw fifty-five thousand people on hot days. A photo shows so many that no sand is visible. The couple probably could not believe their lives would ever be much different—not even when workers dug post holes around him for fences. Then came bricklayers and carpenters sent by Francis Stanley Rickords, apparently the son of a title company official. The Cap'n told them to go home, but the pistol-packing octogenarian calling herself Mrs. Eddy sensed that the end had arrived.

Two men who had spoken to Streeter about buying lots showed up outside his home on December 10, 1918, and then revealed themselves as title company agents. As a handful of policemen crossed into disputed territory, Ma grabbed a hatchet but was disarmed. The workmen tore down what remained of the home, and all their possessions were once more heaped onto the street.

When night came, Ma slept in a lean-to the Cap'n had made from mats, chairs, carpets, mattresses and an old chest of drawers. Wrapped in a fur coat, Streeter sat on an empty wooden box by a bonfire with a few friends. "We'll stay here until hell freezes over," he said with Spot resting in his lap. A woman told the small gathering "Come on, you tightwads. Each of you give the Captain a dollar. I'll start it off with five." No one made a move, and Streeter accepted her five dollars.

She returned the next evening, but by then, the Streeters had moved off the land forever. The title company attached this sign to the lean-to: "Private No Trespassing." No one knows where the couple went, leaving their furniture behind. In 1919 and 1920, they could be seen by the Calumet River, a largely industrial waterway on the South Side. Their home was the *Vamoose*, a former excursion boat known as a "murder craft" because a crewman had been killed years earlier in a quarrel over pay. Sometimes the Streeters docked their ugly vessel at the end of Municipal Pier.[82]

A group of supporters met a few times as the Lake Michigan Land Association, but all they did was check up on Streeter. He would talk to them about carrying on the fight, but with Ma he spoke of death. He was at least seventy-five years old, eighty-three by his own careless reckoning, and never got around to painting *Elma* on the stern of the *Vamoose*. In mid-January 1921, Land Association member Casper Smith climbed aboard for a visit as the boat rested in the Indiana Harbor Canal. The Cap'n was now blind in one eye from a splinter that shot up as he was chopping kindling and had trouble breathing.

George Wellington Streeter—few people knew his first two names—died aboard his houseboat on January 21. Landowners and the city would not let him be buried in the district. But the Grand Army of the Republic, an influential group of Union army veterans, believed in the valor described in his book and decided to bury him in the final home of many Chicago millionaires, Graceland Cemetery on the North Side, not far from the lake. An American flag was draped over the casket at Grace Episcopal Methodist Church on North LaSalle Street. Mourners included attorney William Anderson, who had won Streeter's prison release. Most people in the forty-car motorcade to Graceland were GAR members. The Cap'n's simple grave marker looks down on the sixteen white columns ringing Potter and Bertha Palmer's twin sarcophagi.[83]

Possessing nothing but the *Vamoose*, Ma listened to friends urging her to pursue her husband's claim. She filed a suit against all the landowners, but her heart was not in it. When the weather improved, she turned the old houseboat into a floating restaurant, selling hot dogs and soft drinks to strollers at Municipal Pier and acting as waitress if they wanted to sit down. When winter set in, she stayed at the home of her unofficially adopted daughter Annie and her husband on West 38th Street. Though not as heavy a drinker as Maria had been, Ma was sometimes picked up for drunken and disorderly conduct. The *South Bend Tribune* said that "court attaches recall once when she was arrested and offered the Chicago 'Gold Coast' as a bond. 'I'm worth several millions,' she told the court officials, 'but I haven't any of it right handy just now.'"[84]

At the frosty end of autumn, she maneuvered the boat into a two-foot-deep artificial channel off Illinois Street, near the pier. The city claimed she had actually moored at the Ogden Slip, 150 feet away, a lie. She boarded up the *Vamoose* and returned to Annie and her husband. The next summer, something happened that made the homebody vow revenge on all the millionaires and all the institutions benefiting from the Streeterville development.

Her boat went against the image of Chicago as a progressive city at a time when Mayor Thompson was staging a "Pageant of Progress" at the pier, and corrupt "Big Bill" may have arranged a shoreline accident. On August 31, 1922, a city-owned boat knocked against the *Vamoose* in its berth of slushy sand and mud. The repairs were not made to Ma's satisfaction, and she alleged that the captain of the city vessel yelled, "To hell with Mrs. Streeter's boat, let it sink, that is what we want it to do." But the *Vamoose* was as unsinkable in its berth as it was unsailable. The craft merely resettled a few feet below the surface.

Using Ma as a figurehead, twenty get-rich-quick investors claiming to be agents of the late Maria's children and therefore Streeter heirs incorporated as a legal body in Phoenix, Arizona, to avoid scrutiny by the Illinois attorney general and paying a hefty state fee. Represented by state senator James Hamilton Lewis, they filed an ejection suit in October against all Gold Coast property owners. Ma announced that she would erect a modern utopia once the most expensive homes in the city were demolished. The investment plan was to issue stock and raise $5 million. But on May 21, 1924, the Illinois Securities Commission declared the venture an illegal "blue sky" operation, since its fraudulent backers were unlicensed.[85]

On her own, she filed a suit that November alleging that for years the city had engaged in activities from "petty larceny to murder [the Kirk killing], to embarrass, terrorize and dispose of this affiant and to destroy her home whether it be a permanent structure or a boat." Ma claimed she owed all north lakefront land as well as its mansions and apartment towers, amounting to $350 million in real estate property. Although a lawyer had her scale down her claim from the Cap'n's 186 acres back to

North Michigan Avenue in 1923. Opening the great bridge to downtown three years earlier made the large-scale development of Streeterville feasible. *Chicago History Museum.*

North Michigan Avenue (from above) circa 1923. Still-undeveloped land can be seen in the far upper right. *Chicago History Museum.*

40 "more or less," Ma sought $100 million in monetary damages against the heirs of Fairbank, Farwell, Ogden, Palmer, Healy and Newberry as well as the Palm Olive Company for its Streeterville office and all institutions and charities receiving rents under arrangements with the original members of the Palmer plan. Judge Hugo Friend dismissed the suit in a single sentence, and on June 24, Ma was charged with creating a harbor nuisance for letting the *Vamoose* stay berthed.

As she persisted in her legal action, the marital troubles of a couple she had never heard of settled the issue. Myles Cannavan of Chicago obtained a dissolution of marriage ruling against Mary or Mamie Collins, the gold-digger who had abandoned the Cap'n in 1905. Circuit Court Judge F. George Rush concurred that Mary had never obtained a divorce from Streeter. This paved the way for Superior Court judge James Wilkerson to rule that Ma, not being a lawful heir, had no standing for her suit. Like all other jurists in Streeter cases, Wilkerson made no ruling on its merits.[86]

A Mrs. Elmira Streeter had entered the courtroom with high hopes of being declared a millionairess, and she left as plain, penniless Miss Elmira Lockwood. A few days later, she abandoned the *Vamoose* and lived on funds sent by her family. The city burned the boat down in 1928. In 1936, when large buildings covered what had been the marsh, Ma was just another charity case admitted to Cook County Hospital to die. She passed away on October 18 at the age of sixty-three and was buried in Elkhart County, Indiana.

Cap'n Streeter died at the moment the land he said he created began rising up in its second life, and there was nothing gradual about it.

PHASE TWO

"THE EXCLUSIVE STREETERVILLE SECTION OF CHICAGO"

Chicago has "developed along no practical, logical lines.
This is a real estate town."
—*Mayor Harold Washington*

15

Property owners in the North Central Business Association took measures in 1918 to keep the former Pine Street from declining as some other residential streets had. They wanted the then named Lincoln Park Boulevard to become the world's greatest thoroughfare by improving the area around it. The first step was distributing a survey asking Near North Siders whether portions confined to mansions should be opened to multiple-family residences. Without Palmer's guidance or a master plan, the association hoped the construction of tall apartment buildings would thwart further plans for factories close to the lake and river mouth. Presenting the survey results to the city council, the business association called for restricting building heights to ten stories and banning any business not in keeping with high-class commercial activities. This meant no saloons, music halls or laundries, sweeping away the Near North Side's past as a haven for runaways, tramps, hookers and squatters. The city adopted most of the recommendations but allowed heights of twelve stories, and quite soon exceptions were granted.[87]

After all, aldermen were finally administering Chicago as a large city rather than an overgrown town. In 1920, Mayor William Hale Thompson with unprecedented ceremony opened the bilevel North Michigan Avenue bridge (now the DuSable Bridge) linking the North Side with downtown and turning sleepy former Pine Street into North Michigan Avenue. The sudden importance of Streeterville was seen in 1922, when the city chose the intersection of North Michigan and Randolph for its first traffic light.

North Michigan Avenue in the 1920s, looking north to the lake. Former Pine Street was becoming the spine for development projects east to Lake Shore Drive. *Chicago History Museum.*

Early '20s zoning changes ushered in a surge in tall residential buildings for what the Baird and Warner real estate firm called "discriminating families" between the lake and North Michigan. Among the new rises was a "flat house" designed by Benjamin Marshall at 199 Lake Shore Drive in the original street numbering. A promotional brochure crowed that this expensive box of a building "is located in the exclusive Streeterville section of Chicago. Being situated on the bend of the outer drive [Lake Shore Drive], its windows enjoy a magnificent sweep of seascape as well as the curving, wooded shoreline of Lake Michigan." Jumping ahead again, after delays caused by the Great Depression and World War II, the city-built Outer Drive merged with the state-built Lake Shore Drive in a modest ceremony on June 18, 1946, making it Chicago's first expressway and weakening Streeterville's exclusivity.

The heightened ambitions for North Michigan Avenue became evident with the grandiose Wrigley Building at the northern end of the new bridge. One of its two linked towers is twenty stories tall, and the other reaches thirty, and their gleaming whiteness comes from a glazed terra-cotta facing to recall the sparkling white buildings of the Columbian Exposition. Construction lasted into 1924, the peak of the city's speakeasy craziness.

The Wrigley Building was immediately followed by the thirty-six-story Gothic Tribune Tower across the street. The structure looks like what a newspaper building should. The two landmark buildings serve as an awe-inspiring gateway to the brand-new district, dwarfing the two columns that welcome visitors to Venice's St. Mark's Square. Also taking advantage of more accommodating zoning laws, the fourteen-story—and later twenty-five-story—Allerton Hotel rose a fecal brown by North Michigan and Chicago Avenues. In those times of straitlaced respectability, the apartment-like rooms were originally grouped in male and female sections.

Among the first tall residential buildings within Streeterville was the Neuville on the Drive at Walton Place, designed by Fugard and Knapp, as many apartment towers in the community would be. The eleven-story Renaissance Revival structure, completed in 1920, had a limestone and brick façade as well as a large lobby giving way to ten-room apartments. Before long, the Neuville was outdone by a twelve-story "flat house" at 229 Lake Shore Drive in the original numbering. Most of its apartments had twelve rooms, not counting four washrooms and three rooms for servants.

Trump Tower (*left*) and the Wrigley Building (*right*). The combination of the old and new lends Streeterville its character. *Photo by the author.*

The one-hundred-story Trump Tower hotel and condo building (*center*), seen from State Street and Wabash Avenue. *Photo by the author.*

A brochure for 936 Lake Shore Drive promises—since no one living near the vast body of water considers it just a lake—"an unrivaled ocean view" along with spacious apartments that architect William Ernest Walker configured for elegant living. Another of his buildings was the Tower Apartments on Walton Place near the historic Water Tower. Walker also designed the nine-story apartment building at 136 LSD, believed the first in the city with a specially built penthouse.

A stone's throw from what had been Streeter's encampment was the Stewart Apartments. Each of its ten flats came with eighteen large rooms and five rooms for servants. But you might have needed a translator to make sense of the blueprints. The floor plan covers *La salle a manger domestiques* (servants' dining area), a *cour ouvert* (open courtyard), an *armoire a linge* (a lowly linen cabinet), a *bibliotheque* (library) and *l'orangerie* protecting weather-sensitive plants. And so it was with 1420, 1448, 1500, 1540....The building at 1540 LSD was sixteen stories high and constructed in French provincial style, with little peaks surrounding a sharp main peak and a disproportionately large chimney. Baird and Warner enthused that "The dignified *porte-cochere* [parking area] accommodates six or eight limousines at one time—ample for any theatre party you may give."

The Allerton Hotel (*left*) across North Michigan Avenue from the City Place and the Omni Hotel (*right*). The new comfortably sits beside the past. *Photo by the author*.

The North Michigan Avenue gateway to Streeterville: the Wrigley Building (*left*) and the Tribune Tower (*right*). The former newspaper headquarters has been converted into deluxe condos. The Hancock Center is in the background. *Photo by the author*.

Chicago may have been at the mercy of bootleg thugs at the street level, but there was now an aristocracy in the sky. Franklin MacVeagh's mansion at 1400 North Lake Shore Drive was torn down for the soaring, poured-concrete Touraine Hotel in 1926. The exterior was faced with brick, limestone slabs and terra cotta. A lobby influenced by Europe had fresco ceilings, marble floors and French walnut paneling. The Touraine kept itself busy with a cigar counter, beauty shop, shoeshine stand, golf instructor, nursemaid service, housemen, waiters, bellboys and a twenty-four-hour switchboard.

Tenants at 1400 would include *Chicago Sun-Times* publisher Marshall Field IV. In modern times, the condominium management provides laundry pickup, dry cleaning service, an around-the-clock doorman and a fitness center. At 1430 LSD, an apartment with four bedrooms, five bathrooms and custom built-ins was listed not long ago at $3.5 million.

Until 1922, the drive and its feeder streets were entirely residential. The first business concern to move onto the former carriageway seems to have been Illinois Insurance, which set up shop in an apartment at 1212 North Lake Shore Drive. Wanting to live close by, an unheard of extravagance for executives in the past, company founder and chairman James Stevens moved into a handsome six-level brick mansion at 1260 North Lake Shore Drive, which last sold for more than $5 million.[88] Stevens's commercial inroad aroused little interest at the time because Streeterville was still considered exclusively residential. But as more businesses moved in, plans for a Streeterville office tower were no longer novel. In 1929, teams of workmen completed the thirty-six-story, art deco Palmolive Building at 919 North Michigan. The heavily advertised company developed a soap made from palm and olive oils and recently merged with Colgate.

The end of the 1920s saw a new criminal court building on the West Side and an opera house downtown as well as new Streeterville office and apartment buildings, but the construction of lofty structures stopped altogether in the Depression era of the 1930s. As a result, Streeterville lapsed into a hodgepodge. As an example, the 1891 mansion at 1250 North LSD was patterned after an Irish castle in contrast to nearby manses and the angularity of apartment towers behind it, and a mansion at 1320 North LSD was ignominiously knocked down for a parking lot. The space was underutilized for years until the firm of Draper and Kramer fought to erect a forty-story monolith over community objections about its planned height. An agreement was reached with the zoning commission, and the apartment building went up largely as intended.

Water Tower Place and the base of the Chicago Water Tower at North Michigan and Chicago Avenues. *Background*: former Palmolive/Playboy Building with beacon. *Photo by the author.*

Though America had been on its way toward establishing a permanent aristocracy in the 1920s, with hollow displays of wealth and marriages only within one's class, the Great Depression replaced it with a stewardship by the upper middle class working with banks and financiers. More flexible ways of funding encouraged innovations in construction methods and materials. From now on, major Streeterville ventures would be built through credit financing, with banks and insurance companies holding the mortgages.

The shaken-up economy needed a smart new lifestyle: maintenance-free apartments and cooperatives depending on elevators instead of roads. The greatest changes were seen along North Michigan Avenue, where run-down small apartment buildings from its Pine Street past were leveled by 1931 for more attractive medium-rises. Budd Schulberg, who would write the movie *On the Waterfront*, remembered that coming upon North Michigan Avenue in the '30s "was like finding a pearl in a garbage can." Some North Michigan buildings started featuring first-floor shops catering to Gold Coast tastes.

Once World War II ended, construction resumed across Chicago except for Streeterville. The area was a collection of wide look-alike boxy brick commercial structures interrupted by surface-level parking lots. Weedy patches called prairies lay dormant until the owners received

Above: Palmolive Building beacon and North Lake Shore Drive at night, circa 1939. The sweep of the beacon proclaimed the city's importance. *Chicago History Museum.*

Opposite: The Mandel Building at North Michigan Avenue and the river before its demolition, circa 1970s. This ugly brick building was typical of structures in Streeterville in the 1930s and '40s. *Author's collection.*

acceptable offers or secured financing themselves. No one felt they could do anything about a scattering of smoky factories that would have horrified Potter Palmer.

The late nineteenth-century glory of Lake Shore Drive was forgotten; Streeterville had become ordinary. Then in 1947 the nation bustled with ideas arising from the postwar boom, and a price drop by steel mills in the Calumet District shared by Chicago and Indiana increased local construction. Among those alert to the opportunities was real estate developer Arthur Rubloff. He was born in Minnesota to an immigrant Russian Jewish jeweler and his wife. After running away at twelve, Arthur became fascinated with the risks and rewards of land speculation. As a young man, he learned real estate well enough to sell space in Chicago's massive Merchandise Mart.

When Rubloff was established, he suggested turning North Michigan Avenue into an American Champs-Élysées by rejuvenating some buildings,

constructing new ones and widening the street into a landscaped boulevard. All the buildings would be of a certain height to present a single vision from the river to Chicago Avenue. Rubloff is credited with calling his conception the "Magnificent Mile," though he may have adopted the phrase from Richard Hart, president of the Greater North Michigan Avenue Association. Hart's widow said Richard came up with the label around 1950 after seeing Los Angeles's "Miracle Mile," Wilshire Boulevard. Although Rubloff's vision was in accord with the 1909 Burnham Plan, the idea generated only lukewarm interest. And so over the next few years, Rubloff's brainchild was only partially realized, but the "Magnificent Mile" name has stuck as if it has been earned.[89]

In the late 1940s, architect Mies van der Rohe offered a glimpse of what Streeterville would be like in our times by designing two similar twenty-six-story glass towers at 860 and 880 North Lake Shore Drive. He called

The former American Furniture Mart on North Lake Shore Drive became the home of Playboy Enterprises in the 1990s. No traces of this boxy style remain. *Author's collection.*

Fourth Presbyterian Church and Chicago Avenue skyscrapers, from North Michigan Avenue. The religious structure was known as "the millionaires' church" while Cap'n Streeter was causing trouble for them. *Photo by the author.*

860 and 880 North Lake Shore Drive, Mies van der Rohe's Glass House Apartments. What were derided as impractical and unsightly became the future. *Photo by author.*

their designs "skin and bones architecture." But most lenders he approached refused to fund the risky project because of its absence of ornamentation. Think of *The Fountainhead*. When money was found and the buildings started rising in 1949, neighbors snidely called them the "Glass House Apartments." Van der Rohe next designed the likewise see-through towers of the Esplanade Apartments close by, at 900–10 North LSD. Seen from mid-distance, the four structures resemble a collection.

The Palmer castle at 1350 North Lake Shore Drive was sold in 1929 to inventor Vincent Bendix for more than $3 million, reflecting the newly rich's disdain for holdovers from the previous century. Wreckers turned the fabled home into rubble in 1950, and whatever was salvageable was sold to collectors.[90] Its place was taken by generically designed twenty-two-story twin residences, together offering 740 units. At the time, the city's most exclusive district remained too exclusive. Some cooperatives were still turning Jews away, but restrictions were being dropped by the late '50s. The last WASP bastion is said to have been the high-rise at 1500 North Lake Shore Drive, where later tenants would include well-liked governor Richard Ogilvie.

A new day was coming—was already here—but the slumping Loop held onto its economic dominance, with its State Street blocks of display windows and lights around movie marquees. But a few major realty companies were taking an interest in Streeterville's aging, cereal box–shaped commercial structures. In one instance, Hugh Heffner turned the Palmolive Building at 919 North Michigan Avenue into the new offices of *Playboy* magazine, but the famous beacon continued turning 360 degrees every night. This was fine when surrounding buildings were below its path, but people who had just moved into upper-story flats and co-ops complained about a shaft of two-billion-candlepower repeatedly sweeping through their windows. The light was turned off in 1981.

Seven years later, Playboy Enterprises moved to the sixteen-story Lake Shore Place building, at 680 North LSD. The original address was 666, giving rise to the legend that Heffner did not want his offices associated with the Number of the Beast from the Book of Revelations. The block-long, 1926 utilitarian structure—originally the American Furniture Mart—architecturally is a square box with a tower in the middle. After *Playboy* pulled out of Chicago, the building was turned into condos, some listing at $1.7 million.

Early in this century, the Draper and Kramer real estate company gutted the Palmolive for more than one hundred condos. Economy models started at $500,000, and larger units went for $10 million on up. Another case of converting an older building was the remodeling of a 1921 cooperative at 232 East Walton, which was spruced up with gray limestone cladding while the rest of the eleven stories remained reddish brown brick. Its twenty modernized units, most containing four bedrooms, sold for up to $1.4 million each even without inside parking.

Some unusual efforts have been made to preserve Streeterville as an island of office buildings and stacked residences with a lake view. While the city was expanding Oak Street Beach in the 1960s, authorities considered sketches for a giant highway overpass with a wall of concrete linking Lake Shore Drive with Magnificent Mile shops, disrupting the lake panorama. *North Loop News* publisher Bud Albanese won a fight to scrap that idea in favor of an underpass. This explains why anyone walking down Illinois Street might suddenly wonder, "Where did North Michigan Avenue go?" It will be over the person's head.

To make buildings from another era more attractive to renters, some real estate companies found ways of giving the grand dames a makeover. The trend saved the former Lake Shore Athletic Club, at 850 North LSD. Its nineteen stories opened in 1927 in the twilight of elegant men's clubs. Investors included William Wrigley Jr. of the chewing gum family; Streeter's friend Francis X. Busch; and two members of meatpacking families, Harold

Swift and Edward Cudahy. Swimming trials for the 1928 Olympics were held in its pool, preparing former North Avenue Beach lifeguard Johnny Weissmuller to win the gold in Amsterdam and sign a *Tarzan* contract.

The athletic club was bought by a company run by the J.P. Morgan family, but the Great Depression forced its transformation into apartments. Northwestern University took it over in 1977 to house graduate students from its nearby campus and renamed the building the Lake Shore Center. But Northwestern fell behind in the maintenance, and in 2007 the former athletic club was marked for demolition. Preservationists protested, and the structure was remodeled for a senior citizen community. After the 2007– 9 recession, the Beaux-Arts-inspired building was refashioned into five hundred apartments, many with floor-to-ceiling windows. Though its 1920s terra-cotta decoration contrasts with modern residential towers nearby, flats were leased for $1,900 to $12,000 a month.

Harry Weese & Associates did its own turnaround with the Medinah Athletic Club, at 505 North Michigan Avenue, a forty-two-story relic from when Shriners International was an important part of the city. The Moorish-inspired building was completed in 1929 but closed in the Great Depression. Inter-Continental Chicago bought the site and spent a dozen years on a $25 million reconstruction. The result, still with Moorish traces,

The Hotel Inter-Continental, one reason why North Michigan Avenue is called the "Magnificent Mile." *Photo by the author.*

has eight hundred guest rooms in addition to seventy-two suites and twenty-three meeting rooms.

All through the 1950s, major residential structures in Streeterville were as spread out as its parking lots. Like many northern cities, Chicago lost its way as neighborhoods fell to the drug culture. Since local politics tended toward homeostasis, no new blood was coming in and private interests had to take the initiative again. "In the 1960s Chicago was the working center of postwar modernism," wrote Jay Pridmore and George A. Larson in their *Chicago Architecture and Design*. As innovations and bold plans enlivened some suburbs, the new spirit excited younger architects who saw how nearly *all* of Streeterville might support high-rises. This concept was so striking in its time that carrying it out required a special kind of imaginative daring.

Consider Jerry Wolman, son of a grocer. As a youngster, Jerry had found ways of advancing himself to make sure he would not work in Pennsylvania coal mines like boys he knew. He relocated to the District of Columbia as a teenager, was hired by a paint store, rose to manager and went on to head a construction firm with three hundred employees. Tireless Wolman then worked with investors to erect various buildings in the capital, with John Hancock Insurance holding their mortgages.

Wolman became a millionaire several times over while still fairly young. After arriving in Chicago at the suggestion of a friend, he grasped the potential of the 800 block of North Michigan Avenue, near the northwestern edge of Streeterville. With some finagling he bought a plot for $5 million, and John Hancock Insurance agreed to lend him $63 million for the city's tallest building at the time, one hundred stories. More than that, when it opened in 1969 the John Hancock Center was Streeterville's first strong challenge to downtown as the most desirable place to live or work.

The glass and black metal symbol of the city, with its distinctive exterior cross-bracing, clearly had not been designed with a T-square; its sides gradually slope upward and take the eye with them, as with the Eiffel Tower. "The Hancock" is not beautiful but suggests strength and a strident spirit. Inside are restaurants, numerous offices and seven hundred condominiums. People were so excited about the Hancock that the first residents moved in before construction was completed. But within two years, the tower possessed a mystery. Pretty Lorraine Kowalski crashed to her death through a double-pane window in the ninetieth story apartment of a businessman at four o'clock in the morning. Circumstances were never adequately explained, and no one was charged.[91]

The John Hancock Center nearing completion on North Michigan Avenue in 1968. Lake Point Tower is in the upper right. Behind it is the city's water filtration plant and the twin tubes of Navy Pier. *Chicago History Museum.*

As the early development of Lake Shore Drive drained other mansion districts, the upstart area now pulled ever more businesses from the Loop. The traditional downtown still offered travel convenience and tradition, but it was crowded and had almost no residential space. In contrast, North Michigan Avenue and its Streeterville side streets provided thousands of apartments and condos along with leisurely ground-level shopping and the city's first vertical mall, Water Tower Place.

At 859 feet, the mall was the tallest reinforced concrete building in the world when it opened in 1976 near the Hancock Center and across from the historic Water Tower. Its shiny white façade led one critic to describe Water Tower Place's style as "men's room modern." Inside the block-long base are the Ritz-Carlton Hotel and an atrium with glass elevators serving eight levels of single-purpose shops. As recognized almost immediately, Water Tower Place firmly anchored North Michigan Avenue as a desired place for finding special items.

A panicky, short-sighted city administration in 1979 tried to revive the Loop against competition from across the river by turning the faded resplendence of State Street into a pedestrian and bus mall, with disastrous consequences. When Mayor Jane Byrne had the sidewalks jackhammered so that State could once more accommodate auto traffic, it was too late. The challenger won the title.

The success of the Hancock Center and Water Tower Place put a twinkle in the eyes of numerous architects and investment firms about utilizing every available space in Streeterville. For years, long-term leases had tied some properties down. But during the construction craze of the 1980s, lease renegotiations kept tower cranes busy lifting I-beams and concrete blocks to every next level.

One danger in blueprinting major buildings costing millions upon millions is falling back on a sameness to lower costs, so any difference stands out. Moderately at variance with its angular glass and steel surroundings is the tall and narrow City Place, at 678 North Michigan. The mixed-use concrete building, completed in 1990, was proud of its blue and originally soft purplish coloration and is topped by an arched design reminiscent of a Palladian window instead of a flatness. Its thirteen levels of offices are above twenty-one floors of luxury suites.

Amid the surrounding construction scurry, the Hancock was in trouble. A real estate firm bought the landmark for $220 million in 1998, and the business portions were sold in late 2006 to a Chicago-based joint venture that could not meet its debts. The landmark was taken over by Deutsche Bank of Frankfurt-am-Main, and the German owners perceived the Hancock as just

The Chicago Water Tower, the Hancock Center (*left*) and the Ritz-Carlton Hotel (*right*). This northern vista of Streeterville combines the old and the new. *Photo by author*.

The Chicago Water Tower and the Hancock Center are symbols of the city, circa 1980s. *Author's collection.*

another acquisition to be divided up. Ownership of the observation deck went to a Paris firm, and a Boston company bought the antennas. Actually, these were classified as "superstructures" because they had many small antennas fastened to them for radio and TV stations. Even the name has fallen. After serving as a symbol of Chicago, the Hancock has been formally rechristened 875 North Michigan Avenue. Catchy, isn't it?

The western edge of Streeterville in the 1980s, with North Michigan Avenue in the center. The building boom had just begun. *Chicago History Museum.*

Streeterville's awakening helped save the city from further decline in the 1960s, when venture capital was going south and west. As part of the new age, Chicago real estate adventurer Jerrold Wexler ruminated about how the Illinois Central was not doing anything with a track bed leading to the Ogden Slip now that the warehouses and small factories around it were gone. The expanse just outside Streeterville had been overtaken by prairie up to North Michigan Avenue. Suppose, he wondered, he built a major apartment building there?

In his low-key way, deal-maker Wexler bought the "air rights" for track land at Lake Shore Drive despite some question about whether the Illinois Central owned anything other than the track bed. With the matter still in litigation in 1963, Wexler completed the forty-story Outer Drive East. The project, now known as 400 East Randolph, started accepting tenants in 1965, a year before the Illinois Supreme Court ruled that IC Industries, the real estate parent company of the railroad, really could sell the air, after all.

Wexler's gamble encouraged construction, especially around North Michigan Avenue. Then a year after completion of Outer Drive East, the city reaffirmed a zoning policy that the lakefront should be preserved for "public accessibility." But the statement no longer contained a provision that

A cloud lowers on North Michigan Avenue. At such times, a "No Visibility" sign is posted at the ticket desk of the Hancock Center observation deck. *Photo by the author.*

any development near the river mouth be for either harbor improvement or railroad use. The long stagnation was over. William Hartnett, of a firm that had built luxury apartment buildings across the country, worked with two Mies van der Rohe–trained architects, John Heinrich and George Schipporeit, for a knock-'em-dead project farther out into the lake than any other Near North Side building. Their Lake Point Tower rises seventy stories from a man-made promontory at 505 North Lake Shore Drive. Though imposing, it seems orphaned between the East LSD and Navy Pier.

Lake Point's design is best seen close up. Windows of the nine hundred units form a waving glass curtain around three *Y*-shaped divisions. The inner core supports nine elevators. The giant edifice usually appears black but looks golden and purposeful when sunrays strike at the right angle. When completed in 1972, the tower had conformed with Potter Palmer's master plan barring any structure from the lakeward frontage of Lake Shore Drive. But after the city straightened the much-damned S curve, Lake Point Tower became peculiarly isolated from residential developments just across the traffic. And so it stands today like a citadel overlooking a peaceful plain.

Despite the solitariness of the massive structure, Lake Point rents were predictably among the highest in the city. Yet in a few years, the tower was

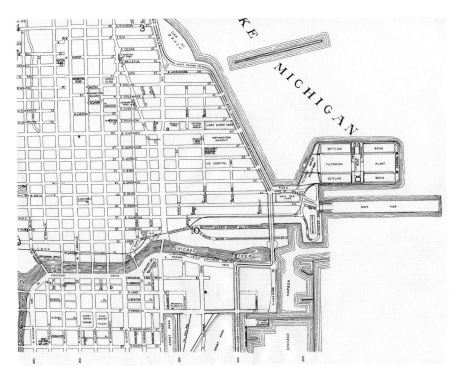

City map of streets in Streeterville. Unless you live or work there, the many short streets of Streeterville can be confusing. *Author's collection.*

vacuuming money from its investors. "Conversion king" Nick Gouletas and his sister, Evangeline, took over and turned the structure into condominiums even though Congress at the time believed the nationwide conversion craze might be squeezing renters out. Nick Gouletas appeared at a hearing and showed that more than 70 percent of his condo buyers had been renters in the buildings.

Also opening in 1972 was Harbor Point, also called Harbor Point Tower, built on landfill over the IC track bed at East Randolph Street. This lies outside Streeterville, but the project had a sisterly relationship with it. The triangular design of the fifty-four-story tower is similar in outline to Lake Point Tower's, but its reflective surface comes from gray-tinted glass and anodized aluminum sheeting used for solar insulation. Residents in Harbor Point's 742 units need not feel stranded; they might go to the hobby room if bored or use its indoor basketball and racquetball courts for recreation. In 2000, the city created small DuSable Harbor to accommodate more than four hundred yachts outside High Point's windows.

Lake Point Tower seen from Oak St. Beach. Its isolation results from a straightening of the *S* curve in Lake Shore Drive and not by design. *Photo by the author.*

The most popular tourist and young-adult location in the city is Navy Pier, at the southeastern edge of Streeterville and sitting between Lake Point Tower and Harbor Point. Mayor "Big Bill" Thompson had pushed the $4 million boondoggle though the city council as a freight terminal and exhibition hall, but suspicion remains that he just wanted to pocket some of the construction spending and exhibit fees. The twin red brick tunnels opened as Municipal Pier in 1916, and from then on it was empty most of the time. Six years later the neglected structure was renamed Navy Pier as a balance to the newly built Soldier Field arena on the Near South Side. In World War II, Navy Pier was used as the base for a training ship with a jerry-rigged flat deck to give recruits experience in taking off and landing on an aircraft carrier.

When the war ended, thousands of young men and women applied for the University of Illinois in central Illinois under the GI Bill's provision for free education up to $500 a year. This forced the state to open a makeshift two-year campus at Navy Pier. Rooms were separated by thin partitions whose gaps allowed students to watch the class next door. Inadequate as the pier was, its alumni included Governor James Thompson, top Chicago policeman Joseph DiLeonardi, mystery writer Stuart Kaminsky, jazz pianist Ramsey Lewis and television newsman John Chancellor.

When a four-year U of I campus opened on the Near West Side in 1965, "Pierniversity" lapsed into an empty ugliness. But attractions were added over the years, an IMAX came and went and a $75 million revitalization gave it new life as a hot visitors' attraction. It now has a specialty food court, shops, a nearly two-hundred-foot Ferris wheel, tour boats, crowds and summertime fireworks. Apart from the Chicago Shakespeare Theater, what the pier lacks in sophistication it makes up for in youthful spirit.

16

To avoid a profusion of cookie-cutter skyscrapers, architects in the 1980s added individual touches more often, such as with the concrete and glass mixed-use high-rise at 441 East Erie. Its transparent atrium connects a twelve-story Mini-Me with a forty-two-story tower. Now called Axis Apartments and Lofts, its original name was the Onterie because of entrances at Ontario and Erie Streets. Axis's greatest construction problem was not the venture's height but its depth. Because the new building replaced a warehouse, crews had to break up a foundation up to twelve feet thick.

Exterior cross-bracing that forms large diamond shapes on one side and *X*s on another eliminated the need for steel beams. Columns on each side of an arch were built with four different strengths to cope with changeable weather near the lake. Noted Bangladeshi American architect Fuziur Rahman Khan died before the building was completed in 1986, but his design won the Best Structure award from the Structural Engineers Association of Illinois. Residents of the 615 apartments could avail themselves of a health club with an indoor pool, a convenience store that never closed, a bank and a dental clinic.

The once deluxe six-story Chandler Apartments of 1910, at 33 East Bellevue Place, was padlocked in 1986 because no one wanted to live in an antique. But Bruce Abrams of LR Development modernized its shell into a dozen condos just two years later. The simple structure is unrelated to the Chandler condominiums across the river, in the tower canyons called the New East Side.

227–37 East Delaware Place is a co-op and apartment building from the 1920s. It is typical of the tastefully simple design of luxury residences in Streeterville. *Photo by the author.*

New York–style co-op at 257 East Delaware Place, once considered the cutting edge in luxury living. *Photo by the author.*

The River Walk off North Michigan Avenue, with the Sheraton Hotel in the background (*left*). If you follow the River Walk to the beach and walk north, you will have seen one of the most beautiful urban sites in America. *Photo by the author.*

Until the vibrant 1980s, the Streeterville story was largely one of individual speculation, whether by Palmer or Wexler. But the dizzying profusion of modern or modernized buildings turned what had been just a *place* into a *community* partly through long-range capital. Visionaries formed investor groups for laying out a quarter mile or more that could be devoted to upscale commercial and residential use. It was as if the Chicago spirit had said that, in the face of declining downtowns across America, it would build an entirely new one on what had once been a bleakness. Little wonder that Chicago planning commissioner Martin Murphy called the general Streeterville area "the most remarkable urban private enterprise success story in the United States."

After the Illinois Central put its air rights up for sale, several investment groups sought options to repurpose the former rail yards. IC Industries went into deep discussions with one of the groups, Chicago-based Metropolitan Structures. Then they brought in another option holder, the Jupiter Corporation, for a massive project that would combine apartment, condo, hotel and business high-rises that would be built in sections over a span of years, each large building maintaining its individuality and carrying its own address. Once again Chicago was a "Make no little plans" kind of town.

For decades, people strived to live on North Lake Shore Drive because of its view of the lake and beaches. But concrete has replaced some of the strand near downtown in a battle with shore erosion. *Photo by the author.*

Mies van der Rohe was chosen to design a breakthrough master plan for Illinois Center that was so bold it would require infrastructure concessions from the city. The overall concept reflected his love for the massive stone buildings he admired before the Nazi takeover. Leaving a Germany gearing for war, van der Rohe regarded Chicago as the place with the most potential, the space and the wherewithal for great structures. His inspiration was fellow German architect Walter Gropius, who stressed "clear, organic forms whose inner logic will be radiant and naked [simple], unencumbered by lying facades and trickeries." In America, van der Rohe became the forerunner of modernism without soulless extremes.

Illinois Center designers did not want to rush the project, setting a thirty-year construction time frame that would allow for replacing older structures in the four-block swath. Mayor Richard J. Daley, known as "the last of the big city bosses," called the newly approved plans the "greatest real estate deal in history." After ground was broken in 1967, the city extended Columbus Drive across the river, and engineers started work on how Lake Shore Drive might be straightened at the S curve to facilitate increased traffic.

As the first structures in Illinois Center rose, friends knew that van der Rohe was smoking himself to the grave. He was awarded the Presidential

Medal of Freedom for his designs of cultural significance before his 1969 death from esophageal cancer. *Chicago* magazine tells us that "family, friends, imitators and enemies" attended his memorial service at the Illinois Institute of Technology in Chicago, long the site of his studio.

Activists feared that what the *Chicago Tribune* estimated as being a $2.5 billion investment would create "a solid wall of buildings cutting Chicago off from their lakefront," but demonstrations could not stop the behemoth. By 2016, the eighty-three acres of Illinois Center comprised five office and residential towers, and three hotels with a combined 3,500 rooms. *Crain's Chicago Business* said more than eight thousand people passed through its doors daily. The separate buildings are linked by an enclosed concourse of shops, bank branches and salons that could use some sunlight.

Vast as it is, Illinois Center has never reached its practically science-fiction early projections. As with many overreaching projects in Streeterville, the complex ran into financial problems as the economy tightened. In 1988, IC Industries was taken over by the Whitman Corporation, operator of an independent PepsiCo. bottling company. Two years later Whitman sold some undeveloped acres within Illinois Center to ease its debt from acquisitions elsewhere. So it has been throughout Streeterville: investor groups that failed were replaced by ones thinking they had a better idea.

In 1982, Chicago's Real Estate Research Corporation found that the city's traditional downtown, that is, the Loop and a few blocks toward the lake, were so overbuilt many office spaces were empty in buildings that had gone up as recently as the 1970s. With the money crunch of the '80s favoring apartment and condo towers over commercial ones, the Near North Side thrived while some cities were hit with construction slowdowns. Rather than let the momentum slacken, one city administration after another since the early '80s has nurtured giant plans by its nearly laissez-faire attitude in promoting economic growth. "The city's attitude toward developers has been 'Come on and build,'" said Elizabeth Hollander of the Metropolitan Housing and Planning Council. "There is a tendency to tell them [architectural firms] 'You're in the business and you know the market. Do what you think is best.'"[92]

The Near North Side extension of Columbus Drive in 1982 opened a fertile region for development once financing could be worked out. As merely a mental exercise, preservationist and architect Harry Weese toyed around with various master plans for the area on his own for twenty years. He said to himself, "There will have to be tall towers there. To pretend otherwise is nonsense because that is the glory of Chicago." But he took no part in its realization.

The once largely underwater barren lots not worth a five-dollar registering fee kept increasing skyward in the community defined as being between Lake Shore Drive on the east and Rush Street on the west, and from the river to Oak Street, with North Michigan Avenue as its artery. In 1988 the Herschfield Companies, a New York real estate and marketing firm, ranked the avenue as the sixth-most-expensive street in the world. All the others were in New York City, Tokyo and Los Angeles. Even so, North Michigan rents were higher than those on London's posh Bond Street.[93]

The mega-development of Illinois Center kindled ideas for something similar. The Chicago Dock and Canal Trust had been withstanding the temptation to sell off its river mouth landfill in sections to hotel and office developers. But then came ideas for a huge real estate venture to be called Cityfront Center. IC trust lawyers entered into a partnership with the real estate branch of Equitable Life Assurance for at last breathing life into fifty acres of former warehouse and industrial land at the disused Ogden Slip.

Planners sought to keep Cityfront Center from the impersonality of Illinois Center not far away. Working with Skidmore, Owings & Merrill of New York, they outlined a number of masonry-clad buildings with separate designs and set back from the street. Total-cost estimates reached $3 billion. Heights were brought into conformity with the general Streeterville vision. At a news conference announcing support for the undertaking, a Metropolitan Housing and Planning Council official said, "If it's all done right it will be good for Dock & Canal and a shot in the arm for [the city's new] downtown. If it's not, we'll all have blown an opportunity that won't come again." The question is, *was* it done right?[94]

The Cityfront circumference is roughly from the lake to North Michigan Avenue and from the river to Illinois Street near the Tribune Tower. The 1985 agreement permitting zoning changes from warehouses to mixed use had called for beautiful new or remodeled buildings, parks, plazas, a riverwalk and decorated streets. But the designs of buildings constructed so far have been unremarkable and the public spaces seem anemic. The *Chicago Tribune* called the project "a cityscape of great expectations and half-kept promises." One imagines that many people passing by are unaware they are in what had been promoted in city council presentations as a fine adornment to the city. But there are some worthy attractions within the project. In 1989, NBC's Chicago offices and studios moved into a thirty-seven-story post–art deco tower at 455 North Cityfront Plaza (545 North Columbus Drive), the style a modern complement to the Tribune Tower of 1925. Among its many leased offices are the Lithuanian, Indian and South Korean consulates.[95]

NBC Tower off North Michigan Avenue houses several embassies. The park has replaced what had been paved, uninviting Pioneer Court, possible location of the home of Chicago founder Jean Baptiste du Sable. *Photo by the author.*

The *Tribune* noted that by 2016 the various standalones of Cityfront Center were already the workplace of more than 4,500 men and women, with additional commercial buildings yet to come. A less ambitious part of the complex is the thirty-one-story Fairbanks condominium building from 2008, built with 280 units. But a less successful segment of Cityfront Center was North Pier at Illinois Street and Lake Shore Drive. The long low-rise hugging the river replaced the 1905 Pugh Terminal exhibition hall at the Ogden Slip in 1990.

North Pier was conceived with quite a buzz as a specialized retail center with street-level restaurants, three tiers of shops and four levels of offices above them, and there was talk about how it would stir the local economy. But its location discouraged patrons: it was too far from State Street and even North Michigan Avenue and with nothing enticing in between. North Pier remained a rejected child even after being dressed up with a new name, River East Plaza, and marketed as Chicago's future Left Bank art colony. After falling into bankruptcy, the building was transformed into the Lofts at River East Center, but its back windows still offered views of the unloved Chicago River.

Also completed in 1990 was the adjacent sixty-one-story North Pier Apartments, renamed 474 North Lake Shore Drive when it was switched to condos in 2005. To set itself apart from its likewise tall neighbors, the façade has pink, maroon and dark gray panels in an abstract pattern. Adding to the confusion of names common in Streeterville, the once-neglected Lofts at River East Center in 2001 became part of a compound including the fifty-eight-story River East Center, at 512 North McClurg Court, its base housing the AMC Theater.

The imposing anchor for all of Streeterville is the formidable Northwestern Memorial Hospital complex, with nearly nine hundred beds in its various buildings and encompassing more than three million square feet, including parking facilities. *U.S. News and World Report* ranked it among the top ten hospitals in the country. Part of the charitable trust Northwestern University received in 1940 came from *Chicago Tribune* publisher Robert McCormick, who wanted the facility used for medical research as well as healing. Construction of the present buildings began in 1994. The Feinberg Pavilion rises seventeen stories, and the Galter Pavilion is twenty-two stories skyward and was where this book was conceived. Over the years, Northwestern Memorial added the Olson Pavilion on Fairbanks Court and the Lurie Children's Hospital on East Chicago Avenue. The buildings are so close together, a second-floor walkway connects them.

The eastern vista of Streeterville, with one of the Northwestern Memorial Hospital buildings in the center (marked NM). *Photo by the author.*

After twenty years in which private initiative alone created modern Streeterville, by 1985, the city's Department of Planning and Development began working with developers and organizations such as the Streeterville Business Alliance to review proposals for replacing disused industrial and dock facilities. The community—once home to squatters and the affluent— at last count had 135 residential high-rises supporting 400,000 permanent residents, qualifying the community as a largely self-contained city. A few more women than men call Streeterville home, and in general the residents are better educated than average. According to Niche.com, the median household in the latest survey was more than $117,000, compared with a national level below $63,000.

Not all businesses on the various levels of Streeterville have signs on their door. As the Cap'n said, "You gotta start with entertainment." Rose Laws and her family knew that to attract high-rollers they would have to do some money flashing of their own. Starting in 1984, they set up eight apartments on the Streeterville streets of East Ohio, Ontario and McClurg, then charged men $200 to $900 for sex with one of their stable of two hundred call girls. All clients were referrals. The lucrative business lasted five years before the "Gold Coast Madam" was raided. Laws pleaded guilty and was sentenced to serve twenty-two months in prison.

The twenty-five-story Allerton Hotel, at 701 North Michigan Avenue, has undergone numerous renovations yet still stands a dull brown, unimaginative structure amid more colorful surroundings. Since 2014, it has been known as the Warwick-Allerton. With this and the 1920 Drake Hotel losing their appeal for many modern-day business-minded visitors, some older buildings have been revamped into plush hotels with amenities. Take the Peninsula Chicago, at 108 East Superior, which boasts that here is where "Far Eastern Graciousness Meets with Midwestern Hospitality." Its exterior is deceptively ordinary except for a pair of marble Oriental lions at the entrance, completely out of character for just-the-basics Chicago. A thirty-story extension rises above building wings, called ells, that resemble arm rests. To fully appreciate its amenities, check into one of its $1,750-per-night deluxe suites. The Peninsula opened in 2001 as part of a mixed-use development and is continually on lists of the best hotels in the country, along with the Langham Chicago near Streeterville.

The Palmolive Building, one of the first large office edifices in Streeterville, still dominates Walton and North Michigan but instead of offices now houses one hundred condos priced generally around $1 million to $6 million. The two upper floors are a penthouse, once owned by actor Vince Vaughn, listed

The lions guarding the Promontory Hotel at Superior and Rush Streets. *Photo by the author.*

at $11.9 million in mid-2021 but sold for $4.9 million less than a year later. The owners of a duplex penthouse on the top two floors of the Palmolive were holding out for $11.9 million.

Since financial structuring is always iffy, there are still a few vacant lots between skyscrapers. Office manager Linda Weissbluth in the 1990s hated seeing the empty plot at 600 North LSD strewn with bottles, so with a $10,000 beautification grant from the Chicago Botanical Garden, she leased the property for a community project. Weissbluth said, "It was a wonderful thing to bring people together. There is so much isolation here." Her garden didn't last long; a developer plowed it under to build a pair of forty-six-story condo and apartment buildings.

Many Streetervillers come from the middle class, but their homes are never distant from those of wealthy professionals, corporate heads, athletes and stock speculators. Residents need not be strangers to one another. Since the 1970s, men and women living vertically have formed organizations fostering community spirit, such as the Gold Coast Neighbors, the River North Residents' Association and the Streeterville Organization of Active Residents (SOAR). Members meet regularly with the Greater North Michigan Avenue Association to express concerns and make suggestions for the city administration. Dwellers also meet individually at such places as a third-story bar and rooftop restaurants.

Nieman Marcus on North Michigan Avenue. Stores like these are reminders that this street was created expressly to serve the wealthy on Lake Shore Drive *Photo by the author.*

Saks Fifth Avenue on North Michigan Avenue. *Photo by the author.*

Typical curves and straight lines along North Michigan Avenue. Streeterville avoids the sameness of some city skylines without having an annoying variety of competing designs. *Photo by the author.*

Burberry on North Michigan Avenue, one of the newer upscale stores on the Avenue. Its crisscrossing exterior design follows the bracing of the nearby John Hancock Center. *Photo by the author.*

By the mid-1990s, Chicago-based urbanologist Peter de Vise, whose findings often met skepticism, reported that the greater Gold Coast of Chicago constituted the second-wealthiest residential community in the United States. Since Beverly Hills, the country's most ritzy area, is a Los Angeles suburb, de Vise's calculations cited the Gold Coast as the wealthiest area within any American city. His two explanations are the lakeshore and closeness to offices and cultural venues. A few years earlier, real estate and accounting expert Jared Shales estimated that the shoreline contributed at least $36 billion a year to the Chicago economy and that 4 percent of jobs downtown (Loop and Streeterville) "wouldn't be there if it weren't for the lake." The percentage no doubt has sharply increased.

Quieter development took place along East Lake Shore Drive, the lakeward bend of the fabled road. Planned and nurtured by architect Benjamin Marshall and others in the late 1920s and early '30s, this portion of Streeterville is even more fashionable than the long northern stretch. Residents have included advice columnist Ann Landers, opera star Claire Dux, Admiral Radio Corporation founder Ross Siragusa, choreographer Ruth Page and Jay Pritzker of the Hyatt hotel chain. Some East LSD residents tend to regard the democratization of wide Oak Street Beach at the foot of the drive with disdain and have been quoted as saying "I wouldn't be caught dead on that beach" and "We live in million-dollar apartments that are right on top of a toilet." Actually, the park district keeps the sands fairly clean, but because so many people use it you might find a candy wrapper or an empty soda pop can here or there.

The city could have lost 75 percent of that beach under plans for a ninety-story hotel on a former industrial site at 600 North Lake Shore Drive. After groups such as Friends of the Parks protested, the city ordered that the design be whittled down to seventy-nine floors, but even then the investors could not raise financing. The Belgravia Group and Sandz Development stepped in and won approval for nearly twin blue flat-sided towers more than forty stories tall. The Streeterville Organization complained that if any more high-rises were built "it's going to be like a canyon here." Opponents fretted that the angular buildings would keep the sun from sunbathers. So the developers used computers to show that at most the towers would cast shadows across just 40 percent of the beach at their longest reach, at 5:00 p.m. in July. An alderman not involved, Bernard Stone, told the complainers, "You act as if this beach belongs to you personally. It belongs to all the people in Chicago."[96]

The concrete and glass condo tower at 990 North Lake Shore Drive combines style and utility. *Photo by the author.*

And so up went the towers at 600 North LSD. When opened in 2009, the four hundred units with one, two, and three-bedroom floor plans sold for $400,000 to $2 million. *Chicago Tribune* architecture critic Blair Kamin described the top of the towers as being concrete walls "that fold with the lightness of origami." Advertising tells us that "the two contemporary forms [towers] emerge fenestrated in ribbons of glass amid a delicate concrete frame, accentuating the panoramic Lake Michigan, Navy Pier and City views. Stacked inset balconies provide added detail to the structures' rhythmic exterior expression."

Built across from small but attractive Lake Shore Park is the twenty-seven-story Residences of Lakeshore Park, at 840 North LSD, essentially a narrow box of a building but with distinctive semicircular glass corner windows at every floor. In 2021, a penthouse there went for $12.5 million. Although General Fitz-Simons reneged on his promise to turn Pearson Street into the garden spot of Chicago, its real estate value keeps up with the rest of Streeterville. A three-bedroom home at 270 East Pearson was sold for $3 million in 2021.

Little attention was given to the cityward bend of the Drive, which had so far resisted the tear-down-and-build rage of the 1980s. Realizing how

Nearly twin towers built in the 600 block of North Michigan Avenue. The towers went up despite community opposition that their shadows would ruin Oak St. Beach across Lake Shore Drive. *Photo by the author.*

Entrance to Lake Shore Park at the eastern end of Streeterville. The park has a playground for children and a fitness track for adults. Too bad most visitors to the area don't know about this restful area. *Photo by the author.*

special this quiet stretch was, the city in 1985 created the East Lake Shore Drive Historic District largely to preserve a park and buildings near the Drake Hotel, at 140 East Walton Place. This privileged section also covers 179–229 East and 999 North LSD. The now-protected structures comprise what dwellers know as "The Block," as if no other one matters. Occupants in this most elegant stretch of Chicago often refer to residences by their address rather than the names developers gave them. So the tall, narrow Drake Tower, unrelated to the nearby hotel, is referred to as the 179 East ("Lake Shore Drive" is understood). That thirty-story building from 1927 was converted into condos in our time. Smaller units cost $590,000 or so, but a full-floor penthouse was priced at $7.5 million. Rents for apartments at 199 and 219 East went for $1,400 to $2,500 a month in the 1980s, depending on size. Some units had vaults for storing furs and refrigerators for garbage to minimize the odor, and a few residents were known to possess telescopes for keeping up with the Joneses. In 2021, a five-bedroom home at 219, built with a fireplace and two private elevators, was offered for $5.1 million.

A story goes that in the later 1920s, the original owners at 209 East LSD wanted to protect their view, so they bought a small structure at the rear, at

210 East Walton, and adapted it into an attractive three-story building for their maids, chauffeurs and other employees. Levels were added over time, and the now five stories house just five condos. Some people at 209 East had Christmas trees delivered atop the elevator to avoid damaging the branches.

"There's something magical about living here," psychiatrist Helen Morrison of East LSD mused in 1982. "This isn't a neighborhood that changes. In a sense, parts of the 1920s and 1930s somehow lasted here…. It's the kind of place where it's not uncommon to run into a couple in full formal dress strolling casually down the street or to see a horse-drawn carriage clip-clopping around the corner with awestruck tourists inside." Dr. Morrison was such an authority on serial killers that she took possession of John Wayne Gacy's brain after he was executed. When residents of the historic East Lake Shore Drive area dine it might be at a fine restaurant inside one of the nearby hotels. After all, "The Block" provides nearly everything they need. At the time of this writing, a three-bedroom condominium at 229 East LSD was listed at $4 million. Its features include a library, laundry room, chef's kitchen and "spa-like bathroom" with fixtures in 18-karat gold.[97]

The fourteen-story jewel in this cluster is the 1920 Drake Hotel, with its more than five hundred rooms and old-fashioned ambiance. Benjamin

Co-op at 209 East Lake Shore Drive. This is part of "The Block" from 179 to 229 East Lake Shore Drive. *Photo by the author.*

The Block. *Photo by the author.*

Marshall designed the hotel, and its name comes from developers John and Tracy Drake. A guest list from the past would look like a roster of Broadway and Hollywood in their heyday, and crime syndicate leader Frank Nitti kept an office here. In 1985, developers Jerry Wexler and Edward Ross entered into a land trust owning the hotel, and in 2005, it was managed by the Hilton Hotels Corporation.

The mid-'80s was for Streeterville and the surrounding area the largest construction wave the city had seen since the aftermath of the Great Fire. Northwestern University's Center for Urban Research and Policy documented this in a study of six adjoining communities: Near North, River North, Streeterville, River West, Loop and South Loop. The researchers found that between 1979 and late 1984, 160 public and private construction projects were completed, 45 more were "in progress" and 50 were on drawing boards. Among the new buildings was a large retail structure at 600 North Michigan that replaced the Baruch Gallery and Jacques restaurant. It now has an AT&T store at the rounded corner and the Grand Lux Cafe on the ground floor.[98]

Stresses arising from high-risk real estate speculation are not usually publicly discussed, but in December 1999 they reached the newspapers. The stories concerned Bruce Abrams, founder of LR Development and the Prism

The Block. *Photo by the author.*

Left: The Block. The eastern end is *North* Lake Shore Drive. *Photo by the author.*

Right: The Block and its park leading to North Michigan Avenue. *Photo by Cathy Klatt.*

Financial mortgage company. He was the man behind the rejuvenation of the Chandler Apartments. Abrams had renovated several other Gold Coast buildings and revitalized the Lakeview neighborhood of the North Side. He took Prism public in May 1999, and its stock value shot up. But he had been worn down by a legal battle over a $250 million Streeterville condominium complex protesters claimed would be too tall for zoning laws, and there must have been other issues troubling him. Abrams stood on the rear balcony of his eighteenth-story condo at the former Mayfair Hotel, at 181 East Lake Shore Drive, and plunged to his death at age thirty-eight.[99]

Just off Oak Street Beach is the W Hotel Lakeshore. A newspaper said a mini-staff of five catered to the specific needs of guests, such as fetching luggage arriving late at the airport, driving to stores as personal shoppers and providing a business executive with a dress shirt when his baggage was in the air. At every table in its restaurant, the Wave, were small binoculars for watching boats in the lake or whatever else you wanted to watch.

The boxlike Lake Shore Plaza apartment building was put up in 1964 on the site of the gaudy but grand Edith McComick mansion at 1000 North LSD. The structure lost its cachet in 2010 when the city decided to change the address of the condo-conversion tower to 130 East Oak Street. Though any place on North LSD in Streeterville still carried memories of its colorful

Hancock Center and Chicago Water Tower at Christmastime, circa 1980s. *Author's collection.*

past, active feeder streets such as Oak convey a more modern way of life. "A Lake Shore Drive address is usually more desirable," observed Jim Kinney of Baird and Warner, "but it [an East Oak Street address] probably means more when a property is originally hitting the market."[100]

Streeterville's success has encouraged developers to rival it with the "New East Side," a stunning achievement just across the river. Buildings there replaced the rest of the former Illinois Central rail yard and a nine-hole golf

Left: The eastern edge of Streeterville by North Lake Shore Drive in the 1980s. *Chicago History Museum.*

Below: Tunnel entrance to Oak St. Beach off North Lake Shore Drive. The artwork keeps the passageway from seeming functional. *Photo by the author.*

This page, top: Oak Street Beach on a mild day. This is the eastern view from windows in mansions and residential towers along North Lake Shore Drive. In the 1950s, this beach was often crammed ankle-to-ankle with families. *Photo by the author.*

This page, bottom: The promontory between Oak St. Beach and Navy Pier adds a bit of scenery. *Photo by the author.*

Opposite: Oak St. Beach. The watchful lifeguard seems to be sitting in front of Lake Point Tower, but the skyscraper is blocks farther from her than it seems. *Photo by the author.*

A skyscraper built just west of Streeterville, seen from North Michigan Avenue. The success of Streeterville encouraged developers to reach heavenward to the immediate west and south of the district. *Photo by the author.*

course and provide views of both the lake and traditional downtown. One of the most prominent structures is the St. Regis, three years in construction before its 2019 topping out. The venture consists of three interconnected towers rising in a step pattern 47, 71 and 101 stories, making it the tallest building in Chicago after the Willis Tower just west of the Loop. A team headed by Jeanne Gang designed the narrow towers to go in and out of plane, as if a snake were crawling toward the clouds. Behind the largely glass walls are 393 condos and 191 hotel rooms, including 33 suites.

The St. Regis "supertall," formerly the Vista Tower, is only part of a monumental project envisioned by the Magellan Development Group to rival if not overshadow Streeterville. Already constructed under the $4 billion mixed-use Lakeshore East master plan are the wide, fifty-seven story Blue Cross Blue Shield Tower and the forty-three-story Swissotel, with a ballroom on the forty-second floor. Additional buildings on the twenty-eight acres covered by the plan are the forty-four-story Buckingham Plaza condo tower; the fifty-six-story Parkshore, with a pool at the top; and the fifty-five-story North Harbor Tower apartment building. But the New East Side is still waiting for an identity of its own. For now, it feels manufactured rather than organic, as Streeterville does.

The St. Regis "supertall" in the New East Side area across the river from Streeterville. Developers hope to outdo Streeterville, but they will never match its character. *Photo by the author.*

The sky touches the towers at Grand and North Michigan Avenues because Streeterville sometimes creates its own weather. *Photo by the author.*

Above and opposite: Statue of Streeter with Spot at Grand Avenue and McClurg Court. The Cap'n seems to be looking across the onetime wilderness and Lake Michigan. *Photo by the author.*

Streeterville is still growing, and not only upward. In March 2021, when Navy Pier was closed by the coronavirus, the Sable Hotel opened its 223 rooms at 900 East Grand Avenue, at the south side of the former exhibition hall. The name came from the World War II Navy training ship USS *Sable*, once docked at the pier, rather than Chicago founder Jean Baptiste du Sable. The hotel has been likened to what a seventy-story building would be when lying on its side. A more recent Streeterville residential building is the sixty-nine-story One Bennett Park Place, which comes with a little park to justify its name. The tall, narrow structure, whose real address is 451 East Grand, is in a style that might be called nouveau New York and uses "mass dampers" of water to reduce the sway in high winds.[101] Apartments are pricey, and condos go for $1.8 million. The Tribune Tower Residences, with amenities such as a pool, was opened in the former newspaper building in late 2021 for condominiums selling between $900,000 and $1.5 million.

Years ago, the city council decided to honor the founders of Streeterville with the names of two streets near their battleground. Short Streeter Drive, designated in 1936, makes a loop at East Grand outside Navy Pier. At least Streeter is spelled correctly, but N.K. Fairbank's name is misgiven in North Fairbanks Court. That short street hosted the twenty-eight-story, award-

winning Harry Weese's Time-Life Building at 541. But the skyscraper was purchased in 2014 for nearly $80 million by Northwestern Memorial Health Center for offices and commercial leasing.

Traveling through the district, you might also see the Cap'n's name on Streeter's Tavern, at 50 East Chicago, and the Streeter apartments, at 345 East Ohio. The area once had the fifty-four-story Streeter Place residential building, at 355 East Ohio, but the name gave way to the Atwater Apartments. At least the Cap'n is represented by David Downes's realistic 2010 statue of him and Spot at Grand Avenue and McClurg.

New structures in the incredible area are probably being drawing-boarded as you read this. Developers will probably keep searching for spaces to support massive Streeterville real estate projects until the last vacant lot and low-rise are gone. How high will they be? Who knows, the sky is the limit.

NOTES

All newspapers are from Chicago unless otherwise identified.

Chapter 1

1. *Herald*, May 30, 1886, checking the ground with poles; de Mare, *G.P.A. Healy*, 223, Healy's lakeshore land.
2. Cook, *Bygone Days in Chicago*, 28.
3. Ambler Scrapbook No. 58, newspaper fragment, no date.
4. *Report of the Submerged* 2:209.
5. *Tribune*, February 1, 1899.
6. Plats for the Canal Trustees Subdivision, Chicago City Hall.
7. Dedmon, *Fabulous Chicago*, 128–29.
8. Brown, "Shore of Lake Michigan," 12–13; *Daily News*, May 16, 1893.
9. Kearney and Merrill, "Contested Shore," 1,103, the park district select committee; *Inter-Ocean*, December 7, 1894, McVeagh and Tree's speaking to lawmakers.
10. *Tribune*, February 6, 1886, Fitz-Simons buying Allmendinger's land.
11. Ambler Scrapbook No. 58, newspaper fragment, probably from the *Tribune*, no date.
12. Ambler Scrapbook No. 59, undated newspaper clipping, Fitz-Simons at park commission meetings; Ambler Scrapbook No. 58, first Lake Shore Drive disclosure.

Chapter 2

13. National Archives, War Department Record and Pension Division, 778764.
14. Ambler Scrapbook No. 58, 107, "intolerable nuisance"; Ballard, *Captain Streeter*, "build a rock wall," 218.
15. Busch, *Casebook of the Curious*, 22, Streeter's "yawl"; Edwards, "My Twenty Year's Experience," privately printed short memoir, "roustabouts"; for the conflict of shore ownership in legal terms, see a federal "bill" filed by Streeter on September 27, 1902, and *Ogden v. Streeter*, filed in U.S. District Court in Chicago on January 5, 1903.
16. Brown, "Shore of Lake Michigan," 8–11.
17. Ambler Scrapbook No. 59, 107, Streeter's second boat, no source given; *Tribune*, September 9, 1890, description of the boat-home.

Chapter 3

18. Bryan, *History of Lincoln Park*, 14.
19. Halsey, *Development of Public Recreation*, 98, special taxing districts; *Bird's Eye Views and Guide to Chicago*; *Commercial and Architectural Chicago*, Handbury and support for Lake Shore Drive.
20. *Daily News*, May 13, 1893, Goudy's persuading the legislature to pass a bill; *Daily News*, May 19, 1893, Shelton's agreeing that the shore owners had determined the LSD route.
21. Brown, "Shore of Lake Michigan," 14–15, ceding land to the park commission and submerged-land deeds; *Tribune*, February 11, 1899, no landfill permit.
22. *Times-Herald*, May 28, 1894, family members in the street inspection division; Brown, "Shore of Lake Michigan," 16, "unconscionable advantage."
23. *Inter-Ocean*, January 23, 1892, Pine Street as an "ignoble lane"; Ambler Scrapbook No. 58; Brown, "Shore of Lake Michigan," 19, "beyond the dreams of avarice."

Chapter 4

24. *Daily News*, May 27, 1893.

25. Brown, "Shore of Lake Michigan," 16, Fitz-Simons' testimony; Chicago newspapers on May 11–14, 1893; *Chicago Herald*, February 24, 1894, Altgeld considered Stockton corrupt.

26. *Daily News*, March 19, 1893.

27. *Daily News* and *Tribune*, May 13, 1893, and fragments in the Ambler Scrapbook No. 59, the Taylor and Pettigrew disclosures, the property owners' list; Kearney and Merrill, "Contested Shore," 1,103, "undue influence…used the Commissioners"; *Globe*, September 12, 1893, "Keep off the grass"; *Daily News*, May 19, 1893, "under the daisies."

28. *Evening Post-Herald* and *Tribune*, November 25–26, 1893. Palmer sent a telegram of outrage.

29. *Times*, May 27, 1894, Moloney's suit to uproot LSD; *Daily News*, May 8–9, 1894, Fitz-Simons barging in. Another account said he just pounded on the desk.

Chapter 5

30. "Piertown," undated article in the Chicago Canal and Trust Company scrapbook; *Herald*, February 20, 1894, questioning Fitz-Simons's dumping at Superior Street.

31. *Daily News*, January 24, 1921.

32. The legislature belatedly authorizes the Drive, see the Lincoln Park Commission annual report of January 1, 1893, 25, and the *Daily News*, March 19, 1893; *Inter-Ocean*, January 23, 1892, the 1892 landowners' meetings; *News*, October 22, 1890, *Inter-Ocean*, May 15 and May 23, 1894, and *Daily News*, May 19, 1894, negotiations with middle-class owners; undated clippings in Ambler Scrapbook No. 59.

33. *Tribune*, November 13, 1891, the fence dispute; Kearney and Merrill, "Contested Shore," 1,089, Streeter's court victory against Fairbank; *Tribune*, September 1, 1891, selling lots; *Tribune*, February 1, 1902, servant girls and laborers.

34. Hoyt, *One Hundred Years of Land*, 214; Mayer and Wade, *Chicago*, 151, 252, South Side land values, land values near the Palmer castle; Busch, *Casebook of the Curious*, 24–25, Calling the land Streeterville by 1892.

35. Busch, *Casebook of the Curious*, 24–25; *Herald-American*, July 9, 1902, Streeter making a business of claiming land.

Chapter 6

36. Kearney and Merrill, "Contested Shore," 1,073, the I-C landfill; Moses, *History of Chicago*, 193–95; *Herald*, April 11, 1893; *Inter-Ocean*, March 30, 1894; Kearney and Merrill, "Contested Shore," 1,103, the U.S. Supreme Court ruling.
37. Wille, *Forever Open*, 71–80, Ward's battle to keep the lakefront for the public; Grossman, "Montgomery Ward," 17; *Tribune*, May 7, 1903, development of Grant Park.
38. Cox, "Origin of Title," the Cox claim; Kearney and Merrill, "Contested Shore," 1095; Brown, "Shore of Lake Michigan," 35; Niles, "Brief History," 19; *Tribune*, January 18 and 21, 1902, and September 25, 1912.
39. *Evening Post*, March 9, 1897; *Sunday Times-Herald*, March 7, 1897.
40. Brown, "Shore of Lake Michigan," 19–24, 28; Kearney and Merrill, "Contested Shore," 1,090–91; *Times-Herald*, March 7, 10 and 14, 1897.
41. *Report of the Submerged*, 10.

Chapter 7

42. *Tribune*, September 21, 1901.
43. *(Elmira) Streeter v. Chicago Title and Trust Company*, 48, warrants against Streeter; *Tribune*, February 8–9, 1893; *Tribune*, February 9, 1893, the great eviction; Bergstrom, "Captain Streeter," 25, renaming the Reutan; Ambler Scrapbook No. 58, fragment, Maria's arrest.
44. *Journal*, March 6, 1893.
45. *Daily News*, January 13, 1894, disclosures of buying and selling among members of the Investment Company; for the plat, see maps for Plat A, E 1/2 SW 1/4, Sec. 3-39-14, Lake Shore Addition to Chicago; *Tribune*, March 2, 1893, allegedly selling lots for $10,000; Ambler Scrapbook No. 58, 107, undated *Tribune* feature, for the Cook County Assessor's Office involvement.
46. *Evening Post-Herald*, March 13–14, 1893.
47. *Tribune*, January 30, 1902, the Cleveland forgery; *Francis Stanley Rickords v. Florence C. Hutchinson*, complainant's exhibit no. 1; *Tribune*, February 1, 1902, that the page did not exist.
48. *Chronicle*, August 29, 1897.
49. "Fishtown," *Tribune*, November 4, 1900.

Chapter 8

50. *Inter-Ocean*, May 5, 1899.
51. Niles, "Brief History," the Declaration of the District.
52. *Inter-Ocean*, May 5, 6 and 7, 1899, the police invasion of the District; Broomwell and Church, "Streeterville Saga," 158–59; *Daily News*, May 6, 1899, "the right to repair yer shore."
53. *Tribune*, May 8, 1899.

Chapter 9

54. *Daily News*, May 26, 1900; *Tribune*, May 28, 1900.
55. *Tribune*, September 21, 1901; *Inter-Ocean*, September 21, 1901.
56. *Tribune*, October 6, 1901.

Chapter 10

57. *Tribune*, October 10, 1901, Maria arrested for kicking windows; *Daily News*, October 2, 1901, Streeter against Mrs. Healy and Mary Cregier; *Tribune*, October 23, 1901, Streeter against Wells.
58. Tribune, December 20, 1901, Ald. Cullerton's building McManners's hut; *Inter-Ocean*, February 13, 1902; *Daily News*, January 31, 1902, Brush denouncing signatures; *Tribune* and *Daily News*, both on February 1, 1902, Brush testimony and Streeter's arrest. Cullerton's reasons for buying lots and hiring McManners were never made clear.
59. *American*, February 14, 1902, Judge Chamberlain's injunction against Cooper.
60. *American*, February 12, 1902, Force's affidavit, Streeter telling his men to shoot.

Chapter 11

61. Ma Streeter's suit against the Chicago Title and Trust Company; McCarthy, *Noblesse Oblige*, 66, Farwell's charities.

62. *Tribune*, June 16, 1902, quashing the fraud indictment; *Daily News* June 30 and July 8, 1902, start of the first murder trial.

63. *Inter-Ocean*, July 8, 1902, Streeter in his first murder trial; *Herald-American*, July 8–9, 1902, cross-examination.

64. *Inter-Ocean*, July 8, 10 and 11, 1902, the first murder trial; *Daily News*, July 8, 9 and 12; *Herald and Examiner*, July 14, 16 and 17, 1902; *Tribune*, July 16, 1902, "Two million dollars."

65. *Daily News*, July 16, 1902, noises from the North Clark Street area.

66. *Tribune*, August 13, 1902, destruction of the McManners shack; *Evening Post*, September 21, 1902, the 1902 eviction.

67. *Tribune*, November 11, 1902, and February 12, 1903, Maria's accident; *Tribune*, November 13, 1902, Streeter in vaudeville.

68. *Tribune*, November 24 and December 4, 1902, the second murder trial and sentencing; *Daily News*, December 3, 1902.

Chapter 12

69. *Chicago Legal News* 36, 268, explanation for Dunne's decision; *Tribune* and *Daily News*, both on November 14, 1904, Streeter freed.

70. *Record-Herald*, June 7, 1905.

71. *Tribune*, November 15, 1915, Ma Streeter described; *Tribune*, July 15, 1907, and October 19, 1936, boat building in South Bend; *Record-Herald*, June 29, 1908, Streeter's 1908 assault arrest; *Record-Herald*, September 12, 1905, Streeterville's "evil name."

72. *Chicago Social Register*, LSD addresses and land values; Moran, *Moran's Dictionary of Chicago*, 202–3; Mayer and Wade, *Chicago*, 252; Hoyt, *One Hundred Years*, 134, 190, 215.

73. *Chicago Legal News*, May 1920, Walker and the beaches; *Evening Post*, October 19–20, 1922, making Oak St. Beach safe for waders.

74. Busch, *Casebook of the Curious*, 42, Streeter fined and his "motor wagon"; *Chicago History Museum Journal* 13, 573; Tessendorf, "Captain Streeter's District," 159.

75. *Daily News*, December 19, 1910, and the *Record Herald* (financial page) and *Tribune*, both on December 20, 1910, the Streeter auction; *Tribune*, July 17, 1910, Streeter's streetcar home; Winslow, scrapbook, 2,612–14

76. *City Club Bulletin* 9, 1913, "child of destiny."

77. B. Kamin, "Unsung Architect Left Lakefront Legacy."

Chapter 13

78. *Daily News*, November 15, 1915; *Tribune*, November 21, 1915.
79. *Daily News*, October 12–13, 1915; *Tribune*, October 13, 1915.
80. *Tribune*, November 15, 1915.

Chapter 14

81. *Journal*, November 13, 1915, and *Daily News*, November 16 and 23, 1915, the Freeman trial; the summation is from Broomwell and Church, "Streeterville Saga."
82. *Tribune*, December 12, 1918, the Streeters on the night of the final eviction; Ma Streeter's 1924 lawsuit, background of the Vamoose.
83. *Daily News*, January 26, 1921.
84. *South Bend Tribune*, October 19, 1936.
85. *Herald and Examiner*, August 8, 1931, fake heirs represented by Senator Lewis; *Tribune*, July 18, 1924, declaration of a "blue sky" operation.
86. *South Bend Tribune*, October 19, 1936.

Chapter 15

87. *Tribune*, October 25, 1922. The plan was to keep a buffer against "businesses," i.e., factories, between Oak and Bellevue, "which," the article added, "opens the entire Gold Coast to apartments and hotels of various heights"; Gapp, "Michigan Avenue," details of North Michigan Avenue development; Stamper, *North Michigan Avenue*, 16, the recommendations.
88. *Tribune*, August 19, 1920, written nearly two years in advance of Illinois Insurance Co. becoming the first commercial occupant on the Drive.
89. *Near North News*, March 14, 1987.
90. Hilliard, "Castles in the Sky."
91. "Printing Executive Quizzed in Death Plunge at Hancock," *Tribune*, August 13, 1971.

Chapter 16

92. McCarron, "Ball in City's Court," "Come on and build" and the recession; Iberta, "Illinois Center Rose Above"; "111 East Wacker (One Illinois Center)," Chicago Architecture Center, https://www.architecture.org.
93. PR News Service (defunct), Chicago, January 1, 1988.
94. McCarron, "Ball in City's Court."
95. B. Kamin, "Cityfront Center Cautionary Tale," "half-kept promises"; Davis, "Chicago's Top Property Ready," "the glory of Chicago."
96. Olivio, "If Condos Get OK," opposition to 600 North LSD; D. Kamin, "Towers Rise to Higher Standards"; Olivio "Money Trumps Sun," the shadows complaint.
97. Cawley, "Easy Street," August 29, 1982.
98. McCarron, "City's Downtown Getting $10 Billion."
99. Wilson and Mendell, "Truly Beloved Developer."
100. "City Hall Tones Down Pair of Tony Addresses," *Tribune*, February 17, 2010.
101. Roeder, "Navy Pier Still Shut."

SELECT BIBLIOGRAPHY

Books

Ballard, Everett Guy. *Captain Streeter, Pioneer.* Chicago: Goulding and Emery, 1913.

Bird's Eye Views and Guide to Chicago. Chicago: Rand McNally and Company, 1898.

Bryan, I.J., comp. *History of Lincoln Park.* Chicago: Lincoln Park Board of Commissioners, 1899.

Busch, Francis X. *Casebook of the Curious and True.* New York: MW Books, 1958.

Casey, Robert J. *Chicago Medium Rare, When We Were Both Young.* New York: Bobbs-Merrill Company, New York, 1952.

Commercial and Architectural Chicago. Chicago: G.W. Orear Publishers, 1887.

Cook, Frederick Francis. *Bygone Days in Chicago: Recollections of the "Garden City" of the Sixties* [1860s]. Chicago: A.C. McClurg Company, 1910.

Dedmon, Emmett. *Fabulous Chicago.* Fairfield, PA: Fairfield Graphics, 1981.

de Mare, Marie. *G.P.A. Healy, American Artist: An Intimate Chronicle of the Nineteenth Century.* New York: David McKay Company, 1954.

Encyclopedia of Biography of Illinois. Chicago: Century Publishers, 1892.

Halsey, Elizabeth. *The Development of Public Recreation in Metropolitan Chicago.* Chicago: Chicago Recreation Commission, 1940.

Horowitz, Helen Lefkowitz. *Culture and the City, Cultural Philanthropy in Chicago from the 1880s to 1917.* Lexington: University Press of Kentucky, 1976.

Hoyt, Homer. *One Hundred Years of Land Values in Chicago*. Chicago: University of Chicago Press, 1933.

Masters, Edgar Lee. *The Epic of Chicago*. Chicago: Henry Raymond Hamilton, Willet Clark and Co., 1932.

Mayer, Harold M., and Richard C. Wade. *Chicago, Growth of a Metropolis*. Chicago: University of Chicago Press, 1969.

McCarthy, Kathleen D. *Noblesse Oblige, Culture and Cultural Philanthropy in Chicago, 1849–1929*. Chicago: University of Chicago Press, 1982.

Moran, George E., ed. *Moran's Dictionary of Chicago and Vicinity*. Chicago: George E. Moran Company, 1909.

Moses, J. *History of Chicago.* Vol. 3. Chicago: Munsell and Co., 1895.

Pegg, Betsy. *Dreams, Money, and Ambitions: A History of Real Estate in Chicago*. Chicago: Chicago Real Estate Board, 1983.

Pridmore, Jay, and George A. Larson. *Chicago Architecture and Design*. New York: Abrams Publishing, 2018.

Report of the Submerged and Shore Lands Investigation Committee. 2 vols. Springfield: Illinois House of Representatives, 1911.

Schulburg, Budd. *Moving Pictures, Memories of a Hollywood Prince*. New York: Scarborough Books, 1982.

Stamper, John W. *North Michigan Avenue*. Portland, OR: Pomegranate Communications, 2005.

Stead, William. *If Christ Came to Chicago*. Chicago: Laird and Lee, 1894.

Wille, Lois. *Forever Open, Clear and Free, the Struggle for Chicago's Lakefront*. Chicago: Henry Regnery Company, 1972.

Wolper, Gregg. *The Chicago Dock and Canal Trust, 1857–1987*. Chicago: Dock and Canal Trust, 1988.

Articles, Periodicals, Scrapbook Collections

Ambler, J.C. (attributed). Scrapbooks No. 58 and No. 59, compiled for the Citizens Association of Chicago, at the Chicago History Museum.

Bergstrom, Edward. "Captain Streeter, Squatter." *Traditions* 4, no. 10 (n.d.): 22.

Broomwell, Kenneth F., and Harlow M. Church. "Streeterville Saga." *Journal of the Illinois State Historical Society* 33 (June 1944).

Brown, Edward O. "The Shore of Lake Michigan." Speech, Law Club of the City Club of Chicago, April 25, 1902.

Cawley, Janet. "Easy Street: Life on Chicago's Most Exclusive Block." *Chicago Tribune Sunday Magazine*, August 29, 1982.

Chicago Dock and Canal Co. 1927 annual report, at the Chicago History Museum.

Chicago Dredge and Dock Co. historical file at the Chicago office of the Chicago Dock and Canal Trust.

Chicago History Museum Journal, no. 13.

Chicago Lawyers file at the Chicago Historical Society.

Chicago Legal News 33, 35, 36, 37, 49 and 57, at the Chicago Bar Association Library.

Chicago Social Register, 1896, Social Register Association, New York, 1896.

Chicago Title and Trust Co. scrapbook.

Chicago Title and Trust file at the Chicago History Museum.

Citizens Association of Chicago scrapbooks, vols. 58–62, at the Chicago History Museum.

City Club Bulletin no. 9, 1913.

Cox, William H. "The Greatest Conspiracy Ever Conceived—Chicago Lake Front Lands." W.E. Johnson, Chicago, 1908.

———. "Origin of Title to the Lake Front Lands." 3 pages. Privately printed, undated.

Davis, Jerry. "Chicago's Top Property Ready for Developing." *Chicago Sun-Times*, October 6, 1982.

Edwards, Levena (Mrs. Eddy). "My Twenty Year's [*sic*] Experience in Streeterville, District of Lake Michigan." N.p., n.d.

Gapp, Paul. "Michigan Avenue: The Promise, the Reality." *Sunday Chicago Tribune*, July 15, 1984.

Grossman, Ron. "Montgomery Ward Deserves Our Gratitude." *Chicago Tribune*, August 10, 2014.

Harpel scrapbook, vol. 5 (1886), at the Chicago History Museum.

Hilliard, Celia. "Castles in the Sky." *Chicago*, November 1978.

———. "Rent Reasonable to Right Parties: Gold Coast Apartment Buildings, 1906–1929." *Chicago Historical Society*, Summer 1979.

Iberta, Don. "Illinois Center Rose Above the Fray, Kept Growing." *Chicago Tribune*, December 22, 1986.

Kamin, Blair. "Cityfront Center Cautionary Tale." *Chicago Tribune*, October 18, 2018.

———. "An Unsung Architect Left Lakefront Legacy." *Chicago Tribune*, January 16, 2011.

Kamin, Don. "Towers Rise to Higher Standards." *Chicago Tribune*, November 23, 2008.

Kearney, Joesph D., and Thomas Merrill. "Contested Shore: Property Rights in Reclaimed Land and the Battle for Streeterville." *Northwestern University Law Review* 107, no. 3 (Spring 2013).

The Land Owner, January, September and November 1887.

McCarron, John. "Ball in City's Court on Plan for Development of Riverfront." *Chicago Tribune*, October 2, 1982.

———. "City's Downtown Getting $10 Billion Shot in the Arm. *Chicago Tribune*, August 21, 1985.

Niles, W.H. "A Brief History and Legal Standing of the District of Lake Michigan." C. Swanberg and Company, Chicago (approximately 1900).

Olivio, Antonio. "If Condos Get OK, Beach to Be a Shadow of Its Old Self." *Chicago Tribune*, September 15, 2004.

———. "Money Trumps Sun on Beach." *Chicago Tribune*, September 16, 2004.

"A Portfolio of Fine Apartment Homes." Baird and Warner, 1928.

Potter Palmer file (five unsigned, brief biographical sketches), circa 1902, at the Chicago History Museum.

Roeder, David H. "Chicago Dock and the Payoffs of Prized Property." *Chicago Enterprise*, November–December 1993.

———. "Navy Pier Still Shut, but Hotel Now Open." *Chicago Sun-Times*, March 18, 2021.

Schroeder, Douglass. "The Issue of the Lakefront, an Historical Survey." (no publisher listed), 1966.

Tessendorf, K.C. "Captain Streeter's District of Lake Michigan." *Chicago History*, Fall 1976.

Wilson, Terry, and David Mendell. "Truly Beloved Developer Mourned." *Chicago Tribune*, December 14, 1999.

Winslow, Charles S., comp. Scrapbook, Chicago History Museum.

Newspapers

Chicago American
Chicago Chronicle
Chicago Daily News
Chicago Evening Post
Chicago Evening Post-Herald
Chicago Globe
Chicago Herald

Chicago Herald-American
Chicago Herald and Examiner
Chicago Inter-Ocean
Chicago Journal
Chicago News
Chicago Post Herald
Chicago Record-Herald
Chicago Sun Times
Chicago Times-Herald
Chicago Tribune

Reports, Lawsuits, Etc.

(Elmira) Streeter v. Chicago Title and Trust Company. Common Law Case No. 403681, Superior Court of Cook County, Oct. 21, 1925, tax fee book 287.

Francis Stanley Rickords v. Florence C. Hutchinson. Cook County Superior Court, March 28, 1917.

National Archives, Pennsylvania Avenue at Eighth Street, Washington, D.C., reference section, military division, for Streeter's military record.

National Climatic Center Environmental Data Service, Federal Building, Asheville, NC, 28801. Cook County Circuit Court. *Streeter, Elma A. v. City of Chicago*, fee book 248–526, chancery court, filed Nov. 14, 1924.

———. Depositions: Complaints Exhibit 1, Superior Court, Francis Stanley Rickords vs. Florence C. Hutchinson et al – George Wellington Streeter v. Francis Stanley Rickords.

———. *Streeter, Elmira v. Chicago Title and Trust Co.*, fee book 287, p. 48, common law, C. No. 403681, filed Oct. 21, 1925.

———. *Streeter, George Wellington v. Ballard, Guy Everett*, depositions, chancery division, fee book 191-554, decree 11-3, 1915

Plat A, E 1/2 SW 1/4, Sec. 3-39-14, Lake Shore Addition to Chicago, Chicago City Hall.

ABOUT THE AUTHOR

Photo by Cathy Klatt.

Wayne Klatt is a retired Chicago journalist who writes about crime and local history.

Visit us at
www.historypress.com